C000276365

West Country
WITCHCRAFT

Roy and Ursula Radford

Peninsula Press

Acknowledgements

The authors would like to record their appreciation and extend
thanks to all those who helped with their research or gave time to
talk of their own experiences, including: the staff of libraries in
Exeter, Okehampton,Wincanton, Launceston, Gloucester,
Dorchester and Taunton; staff in public records offices across the
West Country; Roger King and Liz Crow at the Museum of
Witchcraft; members of the Pagan Association; and, in particular,
Ann and Jerry Sidford, Cassandra Latham and Cecil Williamson.

Published by Peninsula Press Ltd
P.O. Box 31
Newton Abbot
Devon TQ12 5XH

Tel: 01803 875875

Printed in England by The Cromwell Press, Trowbridge, Wiltshire.

ISBN 1 872640 39 7

Contents

Introduction: What is Witchcraft?

Ask this question of both a religious leader, and a practitioner of the 'Craft' as it is known, and their answers will usually conform with one or more of the following:

Witchcraft is. . .

    . . . a great evil that has to be suppressed.

    . . . a wisdom that has for too long has been hidden.

    . . . a tool of the Devil.

    . . . the original religion.

Whichever answer is chosen, it invites further inspection. If witchcraft is an 'original' religion, then there never was, nor is, any 'Devil' associated with it. That particular entity and specific concept of evil was introduced by Christianity, which came late in the compendium of world-wide beliefs.

Two thousand years ago, when Christ came to offer personal guidance to those who would listen, various civilisations and their religions had come and gone.

When the Bronze Age began, two thousand years before His feet could have walked this green and pleasant land, a rich and cultured civilisation was already taking root in the West Country. This civilisation was to become capable of building the great stone circle at Stonehenge, the even greater Temple at Avebury, and smaller sized but no less important stone circles in Devon and Cornwall.

Why these civilised people built such monuments, for what purposes their society used them, and from whom they received guidance, are unanswered questions that have caused immense speculation. Of two things we can be certain: firstly, that the builders had tremendous knowledge and ability; and secondly that they would not have been the only wise ones in the tribe. That wisdom, we suggest, was shared by the Celts, observed by the Romans, and feared for some reason by the Christians.

The 'Wise Craft' existed long before Christianity introduced the Devil to the people of this island.

The Gods of Nature waited while the Wise Craft became witchcraft.

Are the Gods of Nature waiting now for the Wise to return to the Craft ?

1 Celtic Connections with Witchcraft

You were there, but delving into pre-history now is a difficult task to undertake. The 'wisdom' that has become witchcraft was first known and used, 'naturally,' by you in your earliest times. To recover your understanding of your Tribe, of the Moon and the Sun, of Time, and of the Seasons, consider all things with an open mind.

As you seek the grains of truth, let Nature take you on her course.

This was the piece of advice given by a witch over twenty years ago that has led us to take many interesting journeys.

The history of the Celts and their Druids continually attracted our interest. There appears to be very little accurate history to explore. There are today, however, a number of Druidic organisations, each with its own purpose for existence, each offering its own interpretation of Druidism, but all generally guiding the seeker after knowledge towards a reasonable understanding of the past. Direct links between the Druids of over two thousand years ago and the present do not exist but, in the folklore of our nations, the bonds have been maintained. The knowledge that was theirs, is ours for the seeking. The wisdom that was theirs became custom, tradition, and witchcraft.

Druidism was, some say, a philosophy rather than a religion. Others suggest that it was the surviving remains of an early Iberian-Keltic religion. Whatever it was, around it has grown a mythology that includes tales of human sacrifice, bardic culture, blood letting, moon worship, ritual abuse, quaint customs and pagan ceremonies.

Organised religion adopted the route of non-confrontation with its predecessor and placed a veneer of acceptable respectability over long existing custom and practice.

The Celts sought peace in Dumnonia (later known as West Wales) and then Devon and Cornwall. There, and in Ireland, Scotland and Wales, among other independent nations, the Celtic customs found a final home and tribal disintegration ensured their widespread distribution. As the beliefs of the Celtic races were increasingly suppressed, their Druids, male and female, protected their knowledge by passing it on through different groups. The story tellers provide us with mythology handed down by word of mouth with good reason; the bards add philosophy, and the witches add the understanding of natural laws.

In the ancient world, one belief was widespread: reincarnation. It was a belief expressed by Druids and shared by witches.

In the ancient world, life-time was governed by the moon whose reliable and regular appearance and return was witnessed and recorded by the Druids. The moon was vital to witches, and is still relevant to us all.

THE PAGAN CALENDAR

The four vitally important festivals of the Druids are identical to the four great Sabbats of the witches in Celtic countries:

Beltane (30 April), May Eve - Walpurgis Night
Lughnassad (1 August), Lammas
Samhain (31 October), Hallowe'en
Imbolc (2 February), Candlemas.

The equinoxes and solstices celebrated by the Druids became the four lesser Sabbats of witches:

Alban Arthna - the winter solstice
Alban Eilir - the spring equinox
Alban Hefin - the summer solstice
lban Elfred - the autumn equinox.

The eight-part year marks the progression of nature's seasons and these festivals of the Druids and the witches are still celebrated by many more people than just the followers of the craft.

Churchmen and politicians have tried altering the reasons for seasonal celebrations, by appropriating days for the recognition of saints, or workers' rights, making high days and holidays out of others, but they have never managed to remove the real reason for celebration from nature's calendar.

May Day is still celebrated for the coming of summer with singing, dancing, maypoles and merrymaking. Maypoles once stood permanently in many towns, and one, at the appropriately named Paganhill near Stroud in Gloucestershire, was among the tallest in the country, so local people claimed. When Mr Churchill said that fathers were coming home after the war, children, at their mother's bidding, danced around it to celebrate, knowing nothing of its phallic symbolism; not that they would have been interested, as it was the food that came after the performances that they enjoyed, rather than the dancing. We, as children, were dragged along to dance on certain sun days and moon days but, after any of these celebrations and come the night the maypole always seemed bigger somehow, glaring down at us, big enough to scare the living daylight out of some kids, whatever it mean to the Mums. Then, as now, no-one mentioned what the dancing was really all about.

Half a century onwards, when the dark of winter approaches, the witchery of Hallowe'en still gains ascendancy, still providing something to celebrate for young and old. The fertility and planting rites of springtime, and the appreciation of the fruits of the earth at summer's end each have their festivities. Whether it is Christmas, Lady Day, St Valentine's or St Andrew's, the calendar changes made by calculating Romans may have altered the dates, but the celebrations remain as pagan as ever.

The parallels between the beliefs held by the Druids and witches cannot be ignored and, we suggest, the likelihood of common origins passes far beyond being mere possibility.

The likeness of the witches' cauldron to the Sacred Cauldron of Inspiration possessed by the Druid revered Moon Goddess, Cerridwen, is not just a coincidence. The Druid's horned God, Hu Gadarn, is not one to dismiss easily. According to the Bardic Triads it was he who first taught people to use the plough and to cultivate the land and he was the centre of discussion in a letter to Henry VIII's secretary, Cromwell, on 6 April 1538, confirming that pagan worship continued as late as that time in the Diocese of St Asph, in Wales:

> There ys an Image of Darvellgadarn within the said diocese, in whome ye people have so greate confidence, hope, and truste, that they comme dayly a pilgramage unto hym, somme with kyne, other with oxen or horsis, and the reste withe money; in so much that there was fyve or syxe hundrethe pilgrimes to a mans estimacion, that offered to the said image the fifte daie of this presente monethe of Aprill. The innocente people hath ben sore aluryd and entised to worship the saide image, in so much that there is a commyn sayinge as yet amongst them that who so ever will offer anie thinge to the said Image of Darvellgadarn, he hathe power to fatche hym or them that so offers oute of Hell when they be dampned.

The letter inspired the authorities to take action, They burned the image, and a priest of the cult of Darvellgadarn. After centuries that have been filled with the horrors of accusation, torture, trial, and punishment, all without justice being involved or even considered, religious and political intolerance is still widespread. There is an increasing interest in natural laws and many people are taking different paths in search of a philosophy, or way of life, Nature-guided rather than human-inspired.

The spirit of Druidism and the Craft of the Wise are being discovered, revived, and revered by those who proclaim that all who follow the old religions back far enough, shall find their common source, and from that source tread safely on the path ahead.

> Though in the depths of the sunless grove, no more
> The Druid priests the hallowed oak adore;
> Yet, for the Initiate, rocks and whispering trees
> Do still perform mysterious offices.

> William Wordsworth

2 Witches in the West Country

The county of Devon holds the somewhat dubious privilege of having housed one of the first, if not the very first, witchcraft trials, and is now regarded by most historians as having provided the setting, at Exeter's Heavitree gallows, for the last execution in England by the hangman of a woman condemned as a witch, according to law.

As early as 1302 a case was heard in Exeter, at the Borough Sessions, against John de Wermhille, his wife, Agnes de Wermhille and Joan la Cornwalyse of Teignmouth, all of whom were accused of being witches and enchanters who consorted with one Dionysia Baldewyne, in 'unnatural acts'.

By 1311 an investigation into the practice of witchcraft was being undertaken on the instruction of the Bishop of London, but few early records relating to witchcraft have come to light in the West Country, if ever such records existed.

In Somerset it was not until over a century later that allegations of soothsaying and procurement were made against Sir Ralph Botreaux and William Langkelly together with others, unnamed, by Sir William Botreaux. The Botreaux relationship is not defined but Sir William claimed in 1426 that the others had procured John Alwode of Truddoxhill, Hugh Bowet of Kylmington, and John Neuport to participate in acts of necromancy and to conduct magical acts that were intended to weaken, consumé and destroy a living body. The case, brought before a secular court, may have been one that arose from investigations undertaken in the West Country where, in Dorset and Cornwall in addition to Somerset, the commissions appointed were successful in bringing similar allegations to light.

In 1432 a Bodmin man, Henry Hoigges, accused Sir John Harry, a priest and servant to the Prior of Bodmin, of being responsible for his having broken his leg and suffered great hurt. The injuries, according to Hoigges, were caused by Harry's ability to practice evil enchantment and perform wicked sorcery. He further claimed that Sir Harry was boastful about his abilities to bring harm upon him, and that he had threatened that, by some magical means or other, he would break his neck. Fearing that Sir Harry would indeed achieve this aim, Hoigges pleaded with the Chancellor to restrain the defendant from practising such sorcery and witchcraft that amounted to heresy.

Witchcraft had existed in the West Country for centuries, considered as a malevolent influence by religious leaders who were quite prepared to bear false witness against their neighbour.

The biblical teaching, "thou shall not suffer a witch to live", was sufficient to justify the accusations made against innocent victims by corrupt clergymen or lying locals. Women became their main target; particularly the old and infirm, the lonely, and the wise.

The majority brought to trial faced false evidence, accusers that bore them malice, witnesses not known to them, judges who took no notes and who rarely summed up any evidence and, denied the benefit of counsel for the defence, were condemned by a jury that was baying for blood and was prepared to wait a few hours after delivering their verdict to witness the execution of those they sentenced to death. If execution was not immediate, it would be delayed only by a matter of days.

Charges of witchcraft brought against women always exceeded the number of similar charges brought against men in Devon; between 1527 and 1723, 83% of all witchcraft charges were made against women. In Cornwall and Somerset, 75%, and in Dorset, 69%.There was a change of mind in the seemingly more fair-minded Dorset, after 1640. All witchcraft charges brought in the county thereafter, were brought against women.

Devon increased its onslaught against the female sex to 91%, Somerset followed that pattern, to 78%, and only in Cornwall was there a recorded drop, to 73%, in the number of witchcraft charges brought against women. The 'cunning men' of Cornwall it seems were not cunning enough to escape punishment for crimes they probably didn't commit.

During the 17th century, accusations made by one person, or more, against another were not the only way that investigations into the actions of suspected witches were initiated. It is not unusual to find records of the judiciary involved in bringing about such investigations. In Somerset and Dorset *Notes and Queries*, vol i, p 225, a correspondent recalls an order made at the Dorset Summer Assizes held in Dorchester on 10 September 1660. The correspondent notes that the Assizes were probably held late that year, due to the celebrations following the Restoration but that this did not stop the judge from instructing that an inquiry should be made into a case of alleged witchcraft in Sherborne, in the following terms:

> It is ordered by this Court that sr. John ffitz James, knight, Robert Coke Esqre., Thomas Moore Esqre., Walter ffoy Esqrew., and Winston Churchill Esq., ffive of ye justices of ye peace of this county or any two of the doe take care, That the business concerning the witchcraft and consultation with the devill and evill spirits in Sherborne in this county bee with all speede examined, (and any) concerned in ye said business bee by or any two of them bound to the good behaviour. And to appeare att the next Assizes and Genrall Goale delivry to bee holden for this county to answere ye same. And that they alsoe binde over As aforesaid such p'sons of those as by them are to be nowe examined as they shall thinke fitt. And alsoe such prsons to prsecute against them as they shall alsoe thinke (fit) and certifie their said Examinations and Informations att the Assizes.

SIR FRANCIS DRAKE - WARRIOR AND WITCH

The fame of Sir Francis is known wherever England's history is taught and many will know of the legend that promises that, if his drum is beaten whenever danger threatens England, then the great warrior will stir from his grave and return to save his country and countrypeople. In that legend alone there is an indication, one that few will have heard of, that Drake was a follower of the Old Religion. The beat of the drum and the promise of a return from death are not the only indicators, however. During the Napoleonic Wars, rituals were performed to summon Drake and his promised assistance. Between 1914 and 1918 Drake's drum was heard again, and during the Second World War witches gathered in the New Forest to perform ritual ceremonies to secure England's safety when invasion threatened. The witchcraft ceremonies performed at the time of Lammas 1940 were performed solely to achieve a means by which Hitler's expected attack on these islands would be repelled. We make no claims for the success of the witches but no historian has offered an acceptable reason why Hitler didn't invade when his chances of succeeding in conquering this country were at their greatest.

In the West Country, the stories of Drake's ghost are numerous. These are tales of a very active ghost, one that leads a Wild Hunt through wind and storm on dark nights; and the Wild Hunt has undoubted connections with witchcraft. Enemies and friends alike of Sir Francis were convinced that he sold his soul to the Devil in exchange for 'supreme abilities' as a seaman being conveyed to him; it was not long before he was made an Admiral.

It was said that Drake consulted sea-witches off the shores of Plymouth, at Devil's Point, overlooking the entrance to Devonport. According to local legend, it was here, in 1588, that the witches provided him with their help by raising the storms that destroyed the Armada; and it is here that local people claim that the witches still linger.

Because he sold his soul to the Devil in exchange for success, Drake, it is said, can never rest. Perhaps this is so, but, if within every story there is a grain of truth, that truth must surely be that Sir Francis Drake was indeed a follower of the Old Religion.

THE SNOW WITCHES

Snowshill, in the Cotswolds, is arguably among the prettiest of England's villages as it nestles below the hill, its houses tucked around the church and the fifteenth century Manor House. Who would think that this idyllic scene had any connections with witchcraft ?

Charles Wade, a young sapper serving in France during the First World War, was wealthy enough to purchase the dilapidated Manor House when it came up for sale. He set about restoring the property, filling room after room with a collection of oddities, accumulated through his jackdaw interests, many of which revealed and expressed his interests in magic and the supernatural.

While setting out on the road in life at Snowshill that led him to become a pillar of society, and a benefactor to the village, respected by the community, Wade sent a piece of timber taken from one of the rooms to a clairvoyant of his acquaintance in Brighton.

Without knowing its origins the clairvoyant wrote to Wade, telling him that, by holding it, the wood had revealed to her the troubles that a young girl had suffered in the seventeenth century in the house from which it had been removed. She told of the girl's agitation, described her dress, and confirmed her desire to leave the house.

It was some time later that Wade learned that, in 1604, a young heiress, Anne Parsons, had been forced to participate in a marriage ceremony with a worthless fortune-seeker whom she detested. The marriage had been conducted at night but the girl had refused to consummate the marriage on those premises and had left the house and journeyed to Chipping Camden. That unfortunate event had taken place on St Valentine's Night and on the same night during the wild winter of 1881 another girl set out from Snowshill, taking the same route for a similar reason, to avoid a marriage that she feared.

The girl, Joan Turnhill, was perhaps twenty years old and had been in service for almost ten of them. The hard life she led was possibly responsible for her shyness but the way she had with animals, birds and all other creatures made her stand out as being 'different'. She was often seen wandering the hills, sometimes in the company of another. Whether that person was man or woman isn't known but people for miles around attributed the young girl's knowledge of plants and herbs to the tuition she received from witches. Even at a young age, Joan was 'set apart', welcomed when her abilities were needed, shunned when they were not.

Had she been older she would certainly have been regarded as a witch herself, but she was young and pretty. A wealthy builder from London, whose country property was near Moreton-in-Marsh, was attracted to her. She feared that marriage could be forced on her when she learned of his return, his wealth increased apparently by his completion of the demolition of the King's bench gaol in London the previous year.

Snowshill was living up to its name when Joan departed from the village during one of the worst blizzards of 1881. For three days it was not known that she had gone; three days during which the storms never ceased and few people set foot outside their doors. One man who did was a shepherd from Buckland who had lambs to deliver no matter what the weather was like. He had already brought his flock down from the higher hills but as they huddled together as the winds howled around them he decided to put them in a barn. Not unexpectedly, one of the sheep, a black one, was reluctant to be driven into the barn. The shepherd had no trouble seeing its black wool against the snow. He stumbled through the drifting snow after the exhausted sheep, dragging them to barn, where he found the black sheep that had already made its way there.

Secure inside the barn the sheep stayed for another day before the shepherd shovelled away the snow from its door and loosed the bolts. All but four sheep milled about in the barn, disturbed at his coming. The four remained still, beside a young woman who lay near death among them.

In the warmth of the shepherd's cottage the young woman recovered enough to be able to guide the shepherd's wife to concoct a herb potion to speed her full recovery. Neither the man nor his wife questioned the woman before she left their home. They knew that she possessed shape-shifting powers and their great-grandchildren, who now live near Cheltenham, believe that too, with added reason. They also have the knowledge that when their great-grandfather opened his barn that day in 1881, there was no sheep in his flock that bore black markings.

They simply point out that it is well recorded that the powers of witchcraft are passed down from mother to daughter, and that at Snowshill over a century ago, both mother and daughter survived.

A CROSSROADS PRISON
The coven of witches whose members frequented the region around Fairford, in Gloucestershire, was one renowned for showing a malicious attitude towards any traveller who crossed its path. The witches regularly turned Poulton crossroads into a prison for pedlars who passed that way on their way to Cirencester market. As soon as the pedlar, loaded down with a pack, passed the central point of the roads, they would be unable to see any way ahead.

Many travellers reported their experience, saying later that all four exits from the cross-roads had disappeared and they had been trapped inside what seemed to be a light-filled enclosure in which they could walk in any direction they chose. They could only walk forward, however, for a few yards after which, without any effort on their part, they found themselves walking in another direction.

This strange situation of continually walking but getting nowhere would continue until the light of day gave way to evening shadows and, as suddenly as they had vanished, the four roads would appear again. No harm befell those who became spellbound by the witches, but the day was gone and the market would be finished and opportunities to sell their wares would be lost.

Poulton crossroads is also referred to locally as Betty's Grave, the site where a poor girl who committed suicide was laid to rest, buried at crossed roads as a means of containing her restless, earthbound soul until she gained eternal salvation, and her soul could rest in peace.

THE CHARM OF OLD PORTSMOUTH
In 1828 an elderly witch was selling her wares - homemade meat pies and natural preserves - around Portsmouth Point. She came upon the house of a woman who was mourning a lost relative. The witch noted the woman's sombre dress and the expensive ring on her finger and recoiled as if hit by a

blow. Alarmed, the woman asked what ailed her visitor and was shocked when the witch confessed that she had 'seen' that the ring had belonged to a person who now was dead and that it was a ring surrounded by ill fortune.

Only by disposing of the ill-fated object would the woman avoid the misfortunes that the ring carried with it; the witch soon stepped out towards Portsmouth Point with the ring in her own possession. She did so after also convincing the woman that it was necessary for her to purchase one of the witch's pies, for a particular purpose. To ensure that any ill fortune that lingered near her was removed, the woman was instructed by the witch to secure a lock of her hair to the pie with a pin, wrap it up and leave it on the wall of the sea defences some distance from her home. "As the pie doth rot, so passeth away all ill," prophesied the witch to the gullible woman. As soon as the witch departed, the woman did as she had been bid. She summoned her neighbour who helped her lop off a lock of hair. They bound the hair to the pie and hurried to a place near the steps where Horatio Nelson once stood, and left the charm to take its course. The women hurried home without looking back, but others were more observant. The witch, who was waiting nearby, recovered the package, removed the offending hair and pin from the pie which she replaced with her wares, ready for sale once more. It was 'others' you will recall who were more observant. The actions of the witch were observed by the husband of the neighbour who had helped the gullible woman lop her lock of hair.

The watchful man was a magistrate, who, when the witch was brought before him shortly afterwards, was pleased to ensure - with a jail sentence - that any ill-fortune which may have been about Portsmouth Point, was soon suffered by the witch herself.

THE HOUSE AT STURMINSTER NEWTON

The way in which Devil worship has managed to mix with witchcraft, or the wise crafts of old, is perhaps demonstrated in the region around Sturminster Newton. At the southern end of what is now known as Cranbourne Chase the modern armed forces can be found at Blandford Camp, adjacent to the point where three Roman Roads converge close to the ancient site known as the Badbury rings. The whole region is remarkable for its connections with the Old Religion. Witchampton nearby completes a triangle formed with the witches' favoured haunt near Blandford and Badbury. Cerne Abbas and the Moreton Obelisk add further dimensions to the angles of past powers and the region beyond Sturminster Newton is perhaps most aptly named as the Black Moor. Not far distant is Three Legged Cross with its connotations of obvious religious significance conveniently mingling with the more recent association with a three legged place of execution.

When Roman soldiers marched these moors, sites used for crucifixion were placed not far from their camps. In later years the execution style changed to that of hanging the wrongdoer who was unfortunate enough to have been caught stealing so much as a loaf, or food for children.

Hanging, not burning, was the fate of many who practised the ancient crafts in these districts, but corpse candles do burn.

The stories we heard relating to the house in Sturminster Newton that was supposedly used for Devil worship all suggested that the occupants traded their souls to the Devil in return for as little as a torch to light the porch of the house. Trade with the Devil elsewhere invariably concerns long life, wealth, power or glory being bestowed by the Evil One upon the trader, whose soul he shall collect at some specified future time. One story we were asked to accept about the house was that in the 18th century a worshipper of the Devil sold his soul for a candle which he was to light in the porch on two nights each month. That strikes us as not being much of a deal for the Devil but perhaps therein lies a clue to a more reliable reason for the house to have connection with candles.

The new moon and the Full moon are far more significant nights on which candles could be used ceremonially by practitioners of the ancient crafts that existed long before Christianity appeared and brought with it the Devil and all his evil works.

Corpse candles, some made from hands severed from execution victims, feature largely in the folklore of witchcraft and in another story the candles were reported to have been seen after the house had burned down.

The site of the house was obviously significant enough for practitioners of whatever craft was concerned to return to a burned-out building to continue the candle ceremony at two times each month. In a centre where ancient sites are numerous, the craft most likely to have continued in the house at Sturminster Newton so near to the place where corpse candle components could be most conveniently collected is, we suggest, the craft associated with witches.

THE HORRORS OF BERKELEY

Berkeley Castle, in Gloucestershire, was built to defend that area of the West Country from attack by conquerors who came from Normandy. Legend, however, decrees that a fortress was first built on the site, where a convent once stood, by Earl Godwin, who slaughtered the nuns in order to build his castle in the eleventh century. The twelfth-century keep of the castle has wide walls, and within those walls there is a deep well. The familiar of a witch was reputed to inhabit this well. It was a giant toad, and one that consumed humans. As well as being a centre of witchcraft, the castle is one that has witnessed the murder of an English king. In 1327 Edward II was incarcerated there, with the connivance of his French queen, Isabella, who was disgusted by his homosexual appetite for young men. Her hopes that disease would destroy him were not fulfilled and with Lord Berkeley prudently engaged elsewhere, the king's gaolers, Gurney and Maltravers, burst into his cell on 21 September, pinned their prisoner to his bed, and hideously and brutally despatched him with a red-hot iron spit. The screams of the dying king are still said to echo around the corridors of the castle.

Screams that combine with others are still heard penetrating the Severn-side winds that buffet the castle walls where the toad awaits its next meal.

THE POWER OF THE RAVEN

At the time of the Norman conquest there lived a woman in the small town of Berkeley who had given birth, first to seven still-born babes, then to seven sons and seven daughters all of whom survived, but two of whom she despised. That they should live confirmed, to many at the time, that the woman was a witch, but their opinions remained unspoken. Here was no old crone, no flea-bitten hag feared for her unnatural knowledge. The witch of Berkeley was a handsome woman, a rich woman with powerful friends who enjoyed her company, the revelries and feasting she provided, and the comforts she could provide them with. Her familiar was a raven, that she fed with the eyes of men who displeased her.

It was the death of the raven that showed the witch that there were powers more evil than her own. The raven fell dead before her as she sat at her table and she knew in that moment that an eternal age of sorrow awaited her. First, a messenger came running with news that her eldest son and all his family had been slain, then other news of deaths within her family swiftly followed.

Her own powers were diminishing, her friends turned from her. All of her children, and their children, were dead, except the son and daughter she had rejected.

To these two, a monk and a nun, she confessed her wickedness, admitting that her wealth had been given to her by the Devil, in exchange for her soul. Knowing that the time had come for her to settle her debt with the Devil, she pleaded with her children for their help. The monk and the nun agreed to do what little they could to save her soul; saving her life was already beyond them. Their mother died that night.

They wrapped her body in a stag's skin and placed it in a stone coffin which they sealed with three iron chains. The coffin was raised upright, in church, and over it psalms were sung, for forty days. On the third day after that, if the coffin had remained unmolested and the Devil denied access to the body, they intended to bury her in the churchyard, in the knowledge that her soul had been saved.

The forty days passed uneventfully but on the first night thereafter a host of demons entered the church and broke the first chain. On the second night the demons returned, and the second chain was broken. On the third night the demons entered the church again to attack the coffin, but failed to break the third chain. The church shook to its foundations as the hideous demons tried to break the final iron bond. Door panels splintered, doors were raised from their hinges by no human hand and thrown the full length of the building. Sacred statues tumbled unaided into the nave, the pulpit fell and was turned on its side, flagstones lifted and flew through the air. Then a terrible figure appeared among the debris. The figure stood before the stone coffin and called upon the Witch of Berkeley to come to him.

"Follow me, now," was his command.

"I cannot, lord, for I am bound," came the reply.

"I will unbind you," he replied, "to your great loss for defying me." He leaned forward, tore away the chain, and with a single blow shattered the stone.

The screams of the living corpse he pulled from within the coffin filled the church. He dragged the witch out of the church and across the graveyard to where a great black horse stood waiting. The body of this fearsome, hoof stamping, impatient creature was covered in spikes.

The witch's shrieks increased as she was impaled upon them, flung across its broad black shoulders with such force that she was pierced through, the spikes protruding, as the figure mounted the steed. Spurred by the rider the horse leaped forward, and all three, horse, rider, and impaled witch disappeared into the darkness.

Only the blood curdling screams of the witch were to be heard in the night air; just as, sometimes, they still are.

FARINGDON FOLLY

In the second quarter of the seventeenth century the actions of a group of women that took place in the forest outside Exeter, in the area of Faringdon, became something that appears to be known about far from these shores.

A young boy, perhaps no more than ten years of age, had set out from Kilmington, near Axminster, to make his fortune at sea and was making his way across country to seek work with the traders whose ships sailed into the Exe estuary. Tired and hungry as the sun settled behind the screen of trees ahead of him, he was preparing to spend the night alone in the forest, then rise with the dawn choristers to be early at the riverside, when he heard voices. The sounds offered the prospect of food, and a cot for the night so he hastened to locate them but this proved not to be a simple task.

Sounds heard among trees, especially at dusk, have a peculiar way of seemingly coming from different directions. This echoing, almost, of the voices he could hear but not clearly hear enough to easily locate, led him first off in one direction, then another. Around and about among the trees he followed the occasional sounds, that stopped for a while, then began again, until he found himself at the edge of a clearing in which a group of women stood around a tree.

He was about to step forward and greet them when their actions made him cower back into the shadows as a wild fear clutched at his stomach.

He watched from a distance until the horror of what he thought he had first seen was repeated again. The women, obviously witches, were sacrificing young children to the tree, feeding babes in arms into gaping jaws. Jaws that he could see, opening wide, in the trunk itself as it fed on the babies the women offered to it. He ran. His young mind believed that the Devil himself could be at his heels, so he ran, blindly, ignoring the branches that tore open his cheeks as they lashed at him in his flight. He ran until he collapsed, and unconsciousness brought him relief from his torment. Who found him is not known; that he did survive is witnessed in the similarity in versions of this episode that survive not only in England, around the area concerned but also in Holland and as far away as America, in coastal regions where the sea-faring link adds interest.

Conclusions to the tale vary, but all agree that the boy's observations led to a number of women being hounded from their homes after children mysteriously disappeared. In the district, the belief in witches, and the craft, continues.

The last mysterious and unexplained disappearance of a child, Genette Tate, occurred nearby on 19 August 1978, and that case remains on an open file, with the police continuing their investigations.

Overseas, the tale concludes that the women were involved with the abduction, and not the sacrifice of young children. Tales of gypsies stealing children abound in many countries and there is no doubt that what the boy observed troubled him greatly; enough for him to relate his story in later life during his sea-going days perhaps.

Yet there is another possible explanation for what he saw. The ash is one of England's most magical of trees. Widespread throughout the West Country, it has for centuries provided people with protection against witchcraft, and cured their ills. The medical values of the ash tree are legendary. In addition to its leaves being used for poultices, balms, infusions, and in many other ways, the tree itself, according to country folklore, is said to 'absorb' any type of sickness or illness if it is offered the opportunity to do so, and will give up its own life if it fails to provide that help.

Cures obtained by using the ash tree charm have been recorded all over England; and those with the knowledge of that charm, and an understanding of the ash tree's medicinal values, would, in the seventeenth century, have been accused of witchcraft.

How that craft was used for the treatment of children, is clearly recorded, as follows.

A mother, with a son who is ill, takes the child to a nearby wood accompanied by two or three girls, the boy's sisters if possible, but otherwise two virgins.

The women select a young, suitably shaped ash tree, split it open down the middle, and then stand facing each other on opposite sides of the tree. The sick child is, by ritual, placed into the divide of the tree by its mother. After a moment or two, a virgin, on the far side of the tree takes the child.

The women circle the tree and repeat the procedure with the virgin now placing the child into the divided tree.

Three or four times over this is done, with each woman present, in turn, placing the child into the tree to enable the tree to absorb the child's sickness. With the ritual concluded the virgin girls bind the tree up again, to let it heal.

If the tree survives it will have absorbed the sickness, enabling the child to recover, but if the sickness proves fatal for the tree it will also prove fatal for the child and both will die.

Mothers, with their virgin daughters, or assisted by virgin friends, treat a boy child, while the treatment for a girl requires that the father approaches the young ash tree with her, accompanied by two young virgin boys or youths. The tree is split and the males all then follow the same ritual process as the women, passing the child into and through the tree as they conduct the curative charm ceremony.

Did then the boy who became a mariner over two centuries ago witness the witchcraft of healing, or something more sinister in an area where children still disappear?

CORNWALL'S BEAUTIFUL WITCH

The north coast of Cornwall is both beautiful and dangerous. The beauty is obvious to all who are fortunate enough to visit the area. The dangers of the cliffs, and of the seas, are well known to residents who respect them both, and who warn visitors to show respect for them also.

The coast and the seas have changed little since the late eighteenth century when, in one small village, a young fisherman who owned his own boat was the centre of attraction for many a maiden. Owning a boat at so early an age was an obvious indication that the young man possessed great prospects and the attention he had lavished upon him by the maidens in the community, and their mothers, flattered him. He was not a man to let the opportunity for a little dilly-dallying pass by and the high hopes held by more than one mother for their daughter's future enjoyment of life was based upon personal experience. Satisfied by his success at sea, and on land, the young fisherman showed no sign of settling down to marriage, a situation that irritated some of the younger women; but not all.

There was one maiden who appeared to take no interest whatsoever in the young and available man, which made her highly attractive to him but, by continually ignoring his attentions, the young lady made it quite clear that she was not for conquering. Another among the maidens, seventeen years of age, was a witch. Her friends knew that she was already skilled and competent in the craft; her mother and her grandmother had been witches too. None of the maidens would ask the beautiful young witch to help them secure the affections of the fisherman by using the prowess she possessed, because they knew that she was as interested in him as they were. The young witch in fact was quite open about her own affection for the fisherman and went so far one day as to admit that they were soon to marry. The unconquerable girl was among the first to congratulate her and made a point of being on the beach earlier than usual next morning to call similar congratulations to the fisherman as he brought his boat into harbour. The young man shook his head in disbelief. His prospects with this particular beauty were obviously dashed, and he strode off to find the witch.

When he found her he threw discretion to the wind and told her exactly what he thought about her for spreading such unfounded rumours. For all her training, and for all the powers she had inherited from a line of witches, the girl could do nothing to avoid the verbal castigation.

She rushed away to avoid hearing his angry words and from the high cliffs she threw herself into the foaming seas that swirled over the jagged rocks below.

The fisherman's name was carried by the wind along the coast as it broke forth from the lips of the doomed maiden, witch or otherwise, before she sank beneath the foam for the last time.

The other maidens heard her death-torn cry, and some say that it is a cry that can still be heard when death threatens those at sea near that fatal spot. Villagers hurried to help, but of the witch's body there was not a trace, nor has there been since that day. Yet this was a day on which the young fisherman's fortunes changed almost immediately.

With the next tide his nets were almost empty, and what he caught was of little value. From then, his prospects diminished. For no known reason his boat began to spring leaks, his sails were torn in the lightest of offshore breezes, and misfortune seemed to follow his footsteps. Then his parents died within two days of each other, although they had enjoyed perfect health for many years. He became suicidal when the cottage they had all lived in since he was born mysteriously burned to the ground.

The entire village became convinced that, from whatever place her tormented soul was now inhabiting, the witch who had taken her own life was now threatening his. But there were other powers at work none of them could have reckoned with. The maiden who had avoided him, rejecting his interest in her, and whose congratulations given to him had started his troubles, met him one day. Horrified at the haggard appearance of the young man she immediately begged him to allow her help him. For some reason he did not argue when she led the way, at low tide, as they scrambled across the rocks below the high cliffs and collected salt that was drying on the stones. He did not object when she made him turn his back to the sea and throw sun-kissed salt over his shoulder. Nor did he doubt her guidance when she asked him to haul his boat from the water and let it dry out thoroughly.

The newly-made nails she brought to him, to help repair his boat, shone in the sun when she handed them to him, and it was only when he was about to put them down on the ground that the girl uttered any word other than that of encouragement. Screaming for him not to let the nails go, she flung herself forward and snatched them up before they touched the ground.

She then explained that they were maiden nails, nails that were newly made and possessing magical properties because they had never touched the ground.

Whether or not he believed her, the fisherman followed her advice and used the nails to mend his boat, and to fix a horseshoe on it below the waterline.

It could have been a coincidence, but, when he next put the boat out to sea, he returned with the biggest catch he had ever made. From that sailing onwards, the catches he made continued to be valuable, none less than the 'catch' he made of the girl who had helped him and who agreed to become his wife.

The descendants of their family consider to this day that witchcraft was at the bottom of it all and their family fortune was brought to them by a witch; but by which witch, they are not so sure.

WHERE IS THE SHILLINGFORD WITCH?

In the woods near Shillingford St George there once stood a particularly twisted tree that could still be seen until the Exeter to Plymouth road was widened to become a dual carriageway. Of no great height, it was the spectacular convolutions of its trunk and branches that made it a tree that stood out in the memories of all who passed it by. Some still remember the tree and recall being warned in their childhood that to go near it was to invite the witch to carry them off. Needless to say, such warning stories abound but that this one should still be remembered for its particular association with a *witch* is significant; more often that not it is a bogey man who is the threat,

In the Exeter area it was said that there were two witches who loathed each other. One, known as the Shillingford witch, who roamed the woodlands to the south, was the cause of conflict in the district. With her wiles she turned married partners against each other, stimulated strife between neighbours, caused children to fight among themselves, and brought sickness to animals and humans alike. Every misfortune that befell those who lived in the area was attributed to the witch until things got so bad that people moved away, just to be rid of her attentions.

Some, those who decided to fight, sought help from the other witch, who lived and worked in Exeter itself and whose help to the community was well known. Here was a witch who would be regarded as 'white', if such a title held any significance. Witches, like humans, have their own personalities and, also like humans, while some would go out of their way to help others, some would do their utmost to cause harm.

The witch of Exeter knew very well that her opposite number would not easily be stopped from causing trouble across the county, but agreed to try to help the desperate people. She contrived a meeting with her opponent at the time of Beltane, when summer was approaching. In the woods near St George the 'white' witch walked among the trees, stopping now and then to inspect a branch, or newly emerging leaf, and generally gave out the impression that she was busily engaged in some activity associated with nature. The troublemaker watched her, from a distance at first, then came closer and, eventually, when her curiosity could not be contained any longer, she stepped out of the tree to confront her city 'cousin' and demanded to know what she was doing in 'her' woods.

The Exeter witch laughed in her face and told her that the woods were no more 'her' woods than anyone else's woods and if she wanted to look for a tree in which her spirit could reside, at times, she had every right to do so. The Shillingford witch was immediately on her guard. She had no intention of allowing any other practitioner of the craft to take over a residency in her territory.

When the Exeter witch stopped to look at a small, straight, young oak, with obvious interest, the troublemaker instantly settled herself inside the tree and called out that this was her tree, and hers alone. Equally quickly the witch from Exeter agreed with her, and sealed the tree so that the troublemaker could not get back out again. Realising that she was trapped the Shillingford witch thrashed about inside the oak, lashing out with her arms and legs in all directions in a vain attempt to escape. The young oak tree was twisted into knots, but survived the onslaught as, gradually, the witch within lost her will to live. She died in the oak tree, but the tree lived on. Distorted, mis-shapen and twisted, it grew and held the witch until the road widening scheme achieved what the witch could not. The tree was torn down and, as far as we know, destroyed.

But that is the uncertainty. The remains of the witch *might* have been destroyed, but they might have survived, possibly in some piece of furniture. Her trouble-making ways might yet appear again, if misfortune decrees.

WITCHCRAFT AT WOOKEY

The great cave at Wookey Hole near the Somerset town of Wells was formed by the River Axe wearing away the limestone very steadily over a million years or so. Stone Age hunters lived in the caves, the evidence of this being the crude jewellery and pottery found with human remains.

Visitors to the caves today will find the Witch of Wookey standing in the cave awaiting their arrival, as the gigantic stalagmite that is said to be the witch, turned to stone for her wicked ways, has been standing there for thousands of years. Visitors marvel at the formation that can be seen, by some, to be the face and hat of the wicked witch, The witch-like appearance cannot be denied, but the connection of the cave to the Old Religion is something that cannot be dismissed either. The tale that is told of the Witch of Wookey suggests that she lived in the caves with her familiars, a goat and a kid, and that her attempt to seduce a young man from the nearby village was received by him with sheer contempt. Rejected, the witch set out to terrorise the countryside. Animals fell sick simply by being near her, villagers were plagued with illness and ill fortune and even the land seemed to succumb to her will when the crops failed year in, year out.

The frightened people of Somerset appealed to the Abbot of Glastonbury to rid them of their tormentor. He sent a monk to the caves to confront the witch. While evil can triumph when it is allowed to feed on fear, in its eternal combat with the powers of good there is the requirement that truth and justice should be fought for by a clean and honourable soul, if goodness is to prevail. The monk must have satisfied that requirement because the witch, knowing that her evil wickedness would not win the day, fled into the darkness of the caves. The monk, intent on ridding the people of her, pursued the malevolent hag into the bowels of the earth and there succeeded in sprinkling her with holy water. The witch was turned to stone, and stands there now where the conflict ended and the monk left her, all those years ago.

The tale is one which can easily be dismissed, perhaps. England is renowned for tales that conveniently provide an explanation for every misshapen stalagmite, stalactite, outcrop of rock, hilltop, or tor but, in 1912 the Wookey caves were excavated and among the findings brought to light were the remains of a Romano-British woman.

Significantly, perhaps, in close proximity to the body were the remains of a goat and kid, a comb, a dagger, and a rounded object that is described as being 'like a witch's crystal ball'.

THE FLYING WITCH OF YEOVIL

In 1685 a woman was hanged at Chard in Somerset for possessing the power of flight. At her trial, which had taken place the previous year, it is recorded that a witness claimed to have seen the witch offer a 'magic apple' to a boy in Yeovil. Despite being warned of the witch's powers, the boy, according to the witness, took a bite from the apple and then, unaided by any visible means, immediately rose into the air and flew a distance that would seem to have been at least three hundred yards.

THE WHITE WITCH OF EXETER

Living in Exeter in 1851 was a white witch who is often still spoken of right across the county today. His exploits in the districts near Barnstaple, Okehampton and Honiton have been mentioned to us but on one particular occasion he was asked to help a couple who lived near Ashburton. The couple believed that they were being subjected to attack by some kind of evil, and that they had been bewitched by an unknown assailant.

Their crops had failed or hardly flourished for four years, a horse they had bought at market to enable them to plough more ground more easily was fully fit when paraded before prospective buyers but, two hours after coins had crossed from purse to palm, the animal dropped dead in a country lane. A series of incidents took their toll on the health of the fearful couple. Their cow went dry and gave no milk, the goat that they kept as reserve for milk or meat vanished from the meadow beside their home, the good wife was taken ill in April and couldn't complete her spring cleaning before the month was out. This was a serious sign that ill-wishing was occurring for it has long been believed that spring cleaning should be finished before May arrived; or one of the family would die.

Then, the final straw, their cat was delivered of kittens, on May Day. Cats born in that merry month were held in contempt by many Devonians who claimed that the creatures would not catch mice or rats. 'May-chats', the kittens of May, were seldom allowed to live. Their fate was drowning, in the belief that if they survived they would bring 'long-cripples' (vipers), other snakes, slow-worms and, inevitably, a great deal of sorrow, into the house.

The couple swiftly killed the kittens as a way of avoiding further trouble, but nothing changed. Eventually they were forced to call upon a witch from outside the area to assist them in determining the source of the sorcery that surrounded them.

This particular white witch was a man who obviously travelled to fairs and markets across the entire county since his successful exploits and activities are mentioned in areas where these were held. From snippets of information we found in those areas he appears to have been particularly helpful in assisting people plagued with problems that appeared, to them, prolonged if not permanent, and who considered themselves to be in conflict with an evil practitioner of the ancient craft. For the witch-weary countryman and his wife, he was ideal.

Word that they needed his help was despatched up-town by them, carried by a friend who whispered it into receptive ears. The 'wise one' heard the plea, and responded. The 'word courier' returned to the country with the message that the witch had duly agreed to meet the couple in a quiet corner of Ashburton. The message from the white witch had ended with an instruction, "bring with you evidence of ill-doing".

The country couple gathered together the last shrivelled ears of wheat that lay on the floor of their barn, the receipt they had been given for the horse, the severed rope that had once secured their goat, plants from their plot that refused to grow, and many other more gruesome relics of the ills that had befallen them.

With high hopes that an end to their troubles was near, the couple could hardly sleep that night. But their hopes were dashed next morning. Before dawn, the man prepared to make ready the wagon on which they would travel into town. He found its wheel-spokes mysteriously broken. During the dark of night the inexplicable had happened. He had last used the vehicle only the day before, and the wheel-spokes then had certainly been safe, secure and undamaged. Intent on keeping their appointment to meet the white witch the couple would not allow the latest bewitchment to hinder them.

With the evil-touched items of evidence they needed hastily thrust into a sack and slung over his shoulder the man assisted his wife to walk down the rock-strewn, deep-rutted lane towards the town. The Royal Mail coachman had already collected the London-bound letters and packages from the posting house in East Street when the couple arrived in Ashburton. It was past nine in the morning and his mind was taken on how best he could make up three lost minutes before his next stop at Chudleigh. The horses strained beneath his whip as the team set off up the hill. Neither driver nor guard noticed the foot-sore couple who stood to one side as the coach rattled past. Two hundred yards more and the couple were at the Golden Lion, close to where the coach had just departed.

A little late for their meeting they were relieved to find the Exeter witch still waiting, and ignored his remark that "time has as much worth as money on market-day" as they spilled the contents of their sack on the cobbles of the street before him.

Butter-sellers and pie-men passed by while the man glared down at the items on the ground. A lemonade seller decided to seek custom elsewhere as his potential customers watched the witch poke at the rope with his staff, turn a cow-horn around with his toe and, with suitable ceremonial, examine the evidence closely.

The couple watched, and waited . . . and waited. The witch produced a talisman from beneath his cloak, held it out above the items on the ground and then, apparently unsatisfied by his observations, replaced it and drew out another. With his staff he prodded a sow whose piglets had been attracted to the ears of corn strewn around, and as their purchaser thwacked her flank with a birch stave and herded them all out of town the visitor from Exeter considered the alternative talisman before handing it to the woman, with a warning that she must shield her eyes from the charm until moonlight washed over it.

Then, from a purse or pocket, and under cover of his cloak, the witch produced a dark glass bottle containing some sort of medication. This he also handed to the woman, together with written instructions for its preparation. As he did so he ground an ear of evil-touched corn into a white powder on the cobbles beneath his heel.

Seemingly satisfied, he suggested that they should now all repair to the nearby tavern where he would advise them further, and deliver his verdict regarding their bewitchment. He was swift to hold back the man who stepped forward to pick up the remaining pieces of evidence and replace them in his sack.

"Touch not evil," were the white witch's quick words as he made a barrier of his staff, holding it out between the man and the items lying on the dusty street. "Follow me," he added as the pigs turned back to escape the wide wheels of an ox-drawn waggon lumbering down the road towards the town.

The 'wise one' hurried out of their way, with the man and woman in hot pursuit.

It was not until all three of them were seated in the corner of the smoky tavern, supping ale paid for by the couple, that the white witch deigned to speak again.

"Witchcraft, without doubt," he said, as he put down his already half-emptied tankard. He ignored the couple's comment that they had long since decided this for themselves and advised them that for this consultation, the charm, and medication, his fee was two guineas.

The countryman grudgingly pulled the coins from his purse, and paid up. Grasped in a bony hand, the coins disappeared beneath the witch's cloak. He looked around the tavern and leaned forward to avoid being overheard by others. His bony hand reappeared, to be wrapped round his tankard as he quietly advised the couple that while they had been blessed with good fortune by receiving his potion and charm, each of which would provide relief from fear or discomfort, it was unfortunate that they would not know the identity of the witch who had attacked them.

He or she might, he observed, bewitch them again after the benefits of the potion and charm expired. The couple had no need of warning; they had obviously considered that eventuality. It was something he could see written across their worried brows, so the Exeter witch responded to their worries like all such white witches do, without prompting.

He immediately offered, for a trifling guinea more, to practise his art yet further, to peer into his crystal ball and identify the face of the witch whose malevolent acts were the cause of the couple's troubles. The countryman's wife clutched at the maiden nail she had long kept wrapped in her purse and glowed with pleasure at the thought that she might soon learn the identity of the witch whose blood she would then draw with it. The white witch drained his ale pot and banged it down on the table.

"The evil one will surely come," he suggested, then paused as he drew his cuff across his lips. The couple hung on his every word. He would identify the evil witch, he promised them, subject to his fee being found.

"The evil one will surely come," he repeated. "She will come to beg your forgiveness, and your troubles will end."

Once more the countrywoman gripped the maiden nail, and touched the money in her purse. But the money remained there. And neither did her husband make a move to fetch a gold coin from *his* purse.

Had the Exeter witch's suggested threat not become a promise he might have returned home with an extra guinea under his cloak. The canny couple though, well practised in the Devonian art of coin keeping, declined his bonus offer. They were content to wait until their wicked tormentor appeared before them to reveal, by his or her own apology, his or her evil identity.

Thus, simply by waiting to hear those apologetic words, the couple avoided making an unnecessary payment. The witch's pot remained empty and the country couple's departure from the tavern and the town was swift. For their two guineas and the pennies they spent on a jug of ale they took with them the talisman charm, the medicinal potion the witch had prescribed, and a little more understanding about the ways of some witches.

At home that night they followed to the letter the instructions which the Exeter witch had appended to their medicine. With great care they laid out the talisman in the moonlight that filtered through the window and then, tired by the journeys and the long day, they retired to bed.

It seemed that their night-capped heads had hardly rested on the pillows before a noise and commotion startled them. The countrywoman pushed her husband out of bed, fearful of whoever it was who knocked on their door in the middle of the night .

As the man wearily arose and crossed the room to fling open the latticed window his wife clutched the bed blankets to her chin, closely, to avoid the invading air.

"Who's down below?" her husband bellowed. The tone of his voice made his anger obvious. The knocking ceased but there was no reply. An innocent widow who lived nearby, concerned at the couple's absence all day, had been unable to sleep. She had crept from her cottage in the dead of night to ensure that all was well with her neighbours. This charitable lady who had cared solely about their well-being, cowered by the door as the man leaned from the window above and bellowed again.

"Who's there? Show yourself, damn your eyes. I know there's somebody out there. Who is it?" The widow, hiding in the darkness, wished she had not stirred from her own bed. The voice above her came again.

"Wife, bring me my gun." At this, the terrified widow waited no longer. She scuttled away, still hidden by the moonlight shadows.

"I'm sorry, I beg your pardon," she called without looking back. Her voice lifted high on the midnight air. "Please forgive me, I meant you no harm."

The sharp-eared wife, no longer fearful of anything, threw back the blankets.

"Did you hear that, husband?" she cried. "Our forgiveness was requested, begged for indeed; we'll be bewitched no more. The witch's words have come to pass. "

Next day, the finger of suspicion pointed every way at many a woman who may conceivably have been the wicked one. Threats were made, accusations were rife, the constables were called to restore calm among quarrelling neighbours while the country couple considered only the fact that they had been saved from witchcraft, thanks to the white witch of Exeter of course; and the witch's amazing abilities were soon to be known of by everyone they met.

3 Witchcraft in the Landscape

There are hills that attract witches and others, perhaps the most famous of British witchcraft hills being at Pendle in Lancashire. Although it is well outside the West Country area, we mention it only to add a footnote to the great amount that is widely known of that particular hill. On it, in 1652, while the persecution of witches continued, a man with a mission, then as yet unknown to him, walked up to the place where witches worked at their Craft. The man later explained that he visited the witches' hill because he was, "moved of the Lord," to do so and he maintained that during his visit he had a mystical experience, and that he saw a vision. In view of the hill's strong association with witchcraft at the time, it is a wonder that the man was not accused of being a witch himself; but that was not to be. That mystical experience was one that inspired him to undertake the religious mission for which he is remembered and respected. The man on the hill was George Fox, the founder of the Quaker movement.

Turning attention back to the western counties, the hill at Bredon, near Tewkesbury in Gloucestershire, is worth a visit by anyone who has a talent for music or dance that needs to be developed. The remains of an ancient camp are to be found at the top of the hill but, it is the ancient stone that can be found there as well, the Bambury Stone, that holds the link with the witches of the past and present. According to local people, the stone, when touched, inspires or develops artistic abilities. The stone probably derives its name from either the Latin, *ambire*, meaning 'to go round', or possibly from *ambrosie petrie*, meaning 'anointed stone'. Both of these possibilities suggest quite obvious associations with the Craft, and the hill has been possessed of witchcraft connections for centuries. Moreover, even in recent years the possession has been appreciated by local parents who are quite prepared to confirm that their children's abilities with music or with dance were increased and enhanced by occasional visits to the stone. While that social value undoubtedly exists, there is a darker side to the hill's history and connections with witchcraft.

In May 1939 a man named Harry Dean died a mysterious death on Bredon Hill, an event that has remained shrouded in mystery ever since. Harry Dean died in a deserted quarry, apparently killed by strangulation, in a setting that has been reliably described as having been prepared for some sort of ritual, or ceremonial, use. A large boulder had been placed at each of the four cardinal compass points, north, south, west and east. Harry Dean's body was found beside the boulder marking the southern point.

Despite the evidence presented to a hastily convened court, that the man had been strangled, the extremely questionable verdict of 'Accidental Death' was recorded by the Coroner.

Now let our attention turn to Meon Hill, a Warwickshire landmark that some say was created by the Devil while the abbey at Evesham was being built. Opposed to the erection of this saintly place, the Devil expressed his displeasure by picking up and hurling a huge clod of earth. His intention, to destroy the abbey, was thwarted by the prayers of the Bishop of Worcester, St Egwin, who founded the abbey in 717 and who was watching over its building. The strength and sincerity of the Bishop's prayers were rewarded when the missile hurled by the Devil fell to the ground, short of its target, and became Meon Hill. Local legend suggests an early connection between the hill and the Craft, and a report in the *Stratford-upon-Avon Herald* and *Warwickshire Advertiser* dated 16 February 1945 was to lead us to consider continuing probabilities:

OLD MAN'S TERRIBLE INJURIES
Inflicted with Billhook and Pitchfork
TRAGIC DISCOVERY AT QUINTON

Warwickshire police are investigating what may prove to be a murder of a particularly brutal character.

On Wednesday night, following a search, the body of a 74-year-old farm labourer, Mr Charles Walton, of Lower Quinton, was found with terrible injuries on Meon Hill, where he had been engaged in hedge-laying.

A trouncing hook and two-tined pitchfork are said to have been embedded in his body. Mr Walton, who lived with his niece, was a frail old man. He suffered considerably from rheumatism and walked with the aid of two sticks.

A week later the newspaper reported that Chief Inspector Fabian from Scotland Yard had been called in to investigate the case and revealed that the billhook and hayfork that were found embedded in the victim's terribly mutilated body had been used ferociously. The fork had been driven through the man's neck, pinning his body to the ground.

Professor J M Webster form the West Midlands Forensic Laboratory gave evidence at the coroner's court that the cause of death was due to shock and haemorrhage, with grave injuries to the neck and chest, caused by weapons wielded for cutting and stabbing the old man. The inquest was adjourned but, unlike the Bredon Hill murder, there was no doubt whatsoever about the cause of Walton's death.

Chief Inspector Fabian continued his investigations, but the murder of Charles Walton was to become one, among the very few, that remained unsolved by the great detective. In 1950, five years after Walton's murder, the case continued to fascinate Dr Margaret Murray, an 85-year-old Professor of Egyptology at London University. She considered there were more sinister motives for the killing that should be considered: his corpse had been deliberately pinned to the earth with a pitchfork, his throat cut, and his chest slashed with the sign of the cross, all of which gave rise to immediate speculation at the time that witchcraft was involved. These factors, and others, so Dr Murray thought, had been ignored but were the ones that prompted her continued interest. She knew that the body of Charles Walton had been found at Meon Hill on St Valentine's day, Wednesday 14 February, which was also Ash Wednesday. She calculated that this was near Candlemas, by the Old Calendar year, from which eleven days were 'removed' in 1752 when the Gregorian calendar was introduced. Candlemas then, as now, was one of the Great Sabbats celebrated by witches, and at this time of year it is also claimed that the ancient Druids once performed human sacrifice, to encourage field fertility and healthy crops. The connotations connecting the date with her other suspicions helped Dr Murray decide to spend a week or so in the area of the murder, appearing there as an artist at work, sketching the hill, while actually conducting her own investigation into the murder.

Her conclusions, which she later made public, added substance to the early speculation: she considered that Walton had been killed by a person or persons unknown, who held a belief in witchcraft, and who feared the magical power of their victim.

Others point out that, although his blood was violently drawn, this cannot be taken conclusively as proof that his killer(s) considered it vital to destroy his influence and power over them, by taking to bloody extremes in the way that witches had been dealt with for centuries.

Apparently, Charles Walton had possessed the reputation in the region for being a wizard and a practitioner of the black arts.

His murder remains unsolved, but one factor, the ritual use of the pitchfork, remains a reminder to this day for many in the local population of the times when the corpse of a witch was impaled to the earth in exactly the same way, to stop it walking again, after death.

DEATH IN LONG COMPTON

Looking around for further witchcraft connections in the Cotswolds, our attention was drawn to the village of Long Compton, and a killing similar to that of Charles Walton.

In 1875, an elderly lady, Anne Turner, was violently killed in a manner similar to that suffered by Charles Walton, by a man who was considered locally to be mad but who believed that she was a witch and that she had power over him. Anne's murderer, James Heywood, had pinned her to the ground before slashing her throat with two strokes, making the sign of the cross. He claimed that Anne was but one of sixteen witches who lived in and around the village and that by spilling her blood when killing her he had destroyed her evil powers. The case started an outbreak of anti-witch hysteria that left every old lady - and old man - in the region fearful for their lives.

For our purposes, however, while the case confirms the witchcraft connections that stretch through the Cotswolds and the entire West Country, there was another intriguing connection. The geographic relationships of the Meon-Bredon-Long Compton witchcraft murder sites produce another example of the triangles that keep cropping up wherever witchcraft activities occur.

There are many such triangles throughout the West Country that can be explored, but this one has an additional, unusual angle (no pun intended!). Look on a map and you will find that midway between Long Compton and Bredon there is another site to be found strongly associated with witchcraft: Snowshill. With its history of shape-shifting witches, and being a place where the Craft was/is practised, Snowshill adds another dimension to land-laid sorcery.

It creates the witchcraft trinity of Snowshill-Meon-Bredon and the trinity of Snowshill-Meon-Long Compton, and in doing so becomes a finger post pointing across the Cotswolds to other, distant witchcraft trinities that invite investigation by any who will take to the highway to connect with the Craft.

Some might follow the pointer to Glastonbury where, in that beautiful area of Somerset, it said that Joseph of Arimathea established the first church of Celtic Christianity. Some would add that Jesus Christ also walked this land that is sacred to pagan and Christian alike, and that Gwyn ap Nudd, the King of the Fairies and an ancient God of the dead, frequents Glastonbury Tor. Known and named as Woden to the Saxons, Gwyn ap Nudd is said to ride over the hills of Wales and the West Country throughout which he is regarded with dread as the Wild Huntsman. Glastonbury Tor has long been the reputed haunt of witches and a place where witchcraft meetings are conducted at midnight on the eve of specific celebration days. Many occult societies, as distinct from witch cult groups, also regard the Tor as a sacred meeting place.

Perhaps it was the presence of pagan power that prompted the building of a church on the Tor; some attribute to that power the influences that quite literally undermined the church and brought most of it toppling down. A landslide is the official reason given to explain the collapse of the church which, after most of it was destroyed, left only a gaunt tower to provide a dramatic landmark that stands like a giant sentinel pointing to the heavens.

FROM CAULDRON TO CHALICE?

Stories abound that proclaim the Holy Grail as being buried somewhere near Glastonbury. These stories are given credence by the Chalice Well, and nearby Chalice Hill, both of which add to the region's appeal to visitors who seek to know more of such things, and who seek the supernatural. The Holy Grail, however, was not always considered to have the shape of the chalice of Christian convention and is considered by many who follow the Old Religion to have been the Sacred Cauldron of Cerridwen, the Goddess of Nature, and Goddess of the moon. The witchcraft connection, and the use of a cauldron being featured prominently in so many tales and legends relating to witches from all parts of the world, cannot be easily dismissed.

Medea, the witch of Colchis in ancient Greek legend, was a priestess of Hecate, the Goddess of the moon and witchcraft. She used a cauldron and was a member of a coven.

In his book *Greek Myths*, Robert Graves relates that it was with the aid of her cauldron, and assisted by twelve Phoenician bond-maidens, that Medea contrived an evil plot to kill King Pelias. Evil plotting involving the use of a cauldron is of course widely recognised in Shakespeare's accounting of the story of Macbeth, the play feared by actors for its witches' connections.

The transformation of the feared cauldron to the sought-after chalice can be traced through the legends of many countries in which heroes enter strange enchanted realms to follow their quest.

After the coming of Christianity, the Cauldron of Inspiration and Rebirth, with its origins in Celtic mythology, becomes the Holy Grail so nobly sought by the Knights of the Round Table.

Any who consider that a cup cannot command awe and respect, be bravely fought for, and sought by many, have chosen to ignore the custom of giving cups to celebrate achievement in almost every type of competition from football to flower growing. We are perhaps closer to the mysteries of ancient times than we realise when the victorious team raises the FA cup at Wembley and shares its triumph with millions!

Onwards from Glastonbury, in which direction does the next point of the witchcraft trinity appear? Towards Bruton perhaps, and the centre of activity for the Brewham witches, or Yeovil, where their sisters prove the craft. The way is open, the Craft invites us all, and our paths will no doubt cross again, at some future time.

BEWITCHED STONES IN THE WEST

Cornwall is famous for its logan, or rocking, stones, with perhaps the best example to be found at Treryn Dinas. According to local legend, these enormous, finely balanced stones possess the power to turn into a witch anyone who touches them nine times at midnight. The stones are regarded as the meeting place of witches, who ride to them at night on ragwort stems.

Another stone from Cornwall, far smaller in size, is the 'milpreve', a type of prehistoric bead, blue in colour with a wriggly line, sometimes yellow, running through it. The name of the stone is derived from the Cornish 'myl pref', meaning a thousand snakes, which also explains the wriggly line. Water boiled with a milpreve in it is said to be a cure for snakebite. The stone provides a lasting link between Cornwall today and the Druids of the past who, wrote Pliny, wore a bead known as the *ovum anguinum*, the snake's egg, as a badge of office.

The milpreves were later worn in a ring by white witches, or 'pellars', who used to provide written charms for people to use as protection against ill-wishing; a service for which a substantial fee was charged.

Rocks associated with the Devil crop up everywhere, not just in Devon, but it is said he died there, the actual place at which he died being North Lew, according to local legend.

The area is renowned locally for being the rather cold and windy place at which the Devil, during one of his annual visits to Devon caught a cold while collecting souls, expired on Sourton moor, and was quickly buried beneath North Lew village cross to save his intended victims from taking a one-way trip to Hell. Canon Romaine Hervey however, writing about the village in which he was rector from 1919-1938, suggested that some considered the devil to have been a stag that was wise enough to elude hunters for a long time, long enough to become referred to as 'The Devil'. It was this 'Devil' which the Canon believed eventually died in the village square during one particularly harsh winter, providing the population with food, and giving birth to appreciative memories that have lingered on down the years to become legend.

Other local people confess to other foundations for the legend, saying that the 'Devil' was a Cornish 'stag', or fighting cock-bird, that was brought up from the neighbouring county to be engaged in a cock-fight with a Northlew champion.

For some, unknown, reason the Cornish cock mysteriously expired on the night of the fight, which caused rather a commotion among the betting fraternity. Inter-county relationships apparently remained ruffled when the North Lew matrons offered the Cornishmen chicken broth before they made their way back across the Tamar and home to Lostwithiel.

The Devil's Stone, at Sampford Courtenay, in Devil's Lane, is not a local stone. It has upon it the imprint of a foot and misfortune befalls anyone who tries to remove the stone from this ancient track.

There is an altar tomb made of stone in the churchyard at South Molton which has earned a strange reputation. It is suggested that if, on Walpurgis Night, you walk around the tomb three times, then stop and listen, you will hear the Devil who is trapped inside.

Similarly, it is still believed by some local people that if you walk thirteen times around Cabell's Tomb at Buckfastleigh, then place your little finger in the keyhole of the door, you will feel Cabell chewing the finger-tip.

The stone that can be seen beneath an iron seat on the north side of the road going up to St Michael's Church on the hill, at Honiton, is said to be the very stone that was dropped by the Devil when he passed that way, was recognised, and was chased off by local people.

In Dorset, to keep the Devil at bay and ill-fortune away, holy stones were collected and used by the people there for centuries.

Inland, the holy stones were ones that had holes right through them and were sought after by adults and children who worked in the fields. Necklaces and jewellery were made from the stones which when worn, would ensure the wearer's protection from witchcraft, witches and wizards.

On Dorset's coast the stones were similarly believed to afford protection but, rather than to people, it was protection provided to boats. Writing in *Notes and Queries (52)* in 1895, Mr H J Moule, who was Curator of the Dorset County Museum, recalled that when he was a boy it was a common sight to see 'holy flints' being sought along the seashore by scavenging youngsters. These coastal holy stones or, as he described them, sea-rolled flints with a natural bore, were considered to be lucky charms by sailors who would place them in all kinds of vessels in which they sailed on the seas near to home, or far away.

Mr Moule recalled watching a boat-man at Weymouth fastening the charms to the bows of his craft. At Abbotsbury, when boats were pulled up on to the beach, he noted other precautions being taken. On to the rope securing the boat to the beach a holy stone, or beach-holed-stone, was threaded, to ensure that a witch could not climb aboard. When a boat put to sea, and its catch was small when the nets of other craft were filled, the presence of witches would be blamed. Obviously, the basic precautions for protection of the boat while beached had not been observed, the boat was 'witched', and an evil spirit had got on board because a beach-holed stone had not been put in place. To dispel the bewitchment, a mackerel stuck through with pins was placed in the stern of the boat to enable the sharp points to oppose the evil presence.

According to Mr Moule also, the Dolmen on Blackdown is called the hell-stone by local people, for good reason. They suggest that the Devil chucked it there from Portland, some nine miles away.

Devon and Cornwall are renowned for their beautiful moors, majestic cliffs, granite tors, stones that have devilish histories, and stones that can be seen making merry when the time is right.

The rocks of Cosdon Hill, near Okehampton, are said to dance to the tune of the peal when the bells of St Andrew's Church, South Tawton, ring out across the moorland. Up to the hilltop beacon they dance their merry jig, circling again and again where the Celtic midsummer fires once burned, before starting back down the slopes. Walkers, passing those rocks on the day before a moon-lit night, during which the church bells toll, will often notice a difference in the positions of the rocks when they return next day. At these times, when those circumstances apply, the rocks distinctly appear to have indeed moved, returned, but failed to sit again exactly in their previous place in the shape-shifting shadows of Cosdon Hill. These stones, more clearly to be seen on a winter walk perhaps, litter Cosdon hillside like grey confetti thrown about wildly at a giant's wedding, and among them Dartmoor witches pay regular homage to their moon Goddess.

At nearby Belstone, the 'Nine Maidens' to be found on the moor are reputed to be village maids caught, tried, condemned, and then turned to stone as a punishment for the crime of dancing on a Sunday. Legend asserts that their witch-led dancing days are not yet over, for they can sometimes be seen to turn and move when the midday sun rides high above Belstone Tor. Midnight, rather than midday, might be expected to be the time when stones would gain, or resume, a life of their own, but in Devon, darkness is not a requirement before bewitched stones will move.

Grey Wethers, stone circles in the heart of Dartmoor, are said to turn around at sunrise.

Near the site of Moortown Quarry, close to the road from Roseash to Bampton, stands a stone that turns around when it hears a cock crow, while another, in the grounds of Sidbury Manor, still maintains its reputation, referred to by Hutchinson in his *Guide to Sidmouth* almost a century ago, for turning around three times at midday when it hears the clock strike twelve.

On Denbury Down, there is a great boulder to be found that is said to dance at noon.

Local people tell stories of many stones and circles that display the ability to move, walk or magically dance. The test is try to see it happen yourself. With the sun overhead at noon, or the moon on high at midnight, pause beside a standing stone on Dartmoor, at the side of a stone row, or outside a circle, and observe closely the location of the stones. Turn away, look into the distance for ten seconds and take three paces forward before turning back. If the stones are not where you observed them to be, fleeting seconds earlier, you too will have experienced their ability to move.

A qualified 'ologist' of some description would, no doubt, rationalise the experience as something that happens to the human mind when it is affected by heat haze or moonlight, but they are unlikely to have ever walked the moors during any of the seasonal changes, spoken with a sculptor of what can be seen within a rock by those who have eyes to see, or sought personal experience of the bewitching powers of rock. For many who try, their personal experience will defy academic supposition, when rocks revolve or move before their own eyes; or make their presence felt in other mysterious ways.

THE WITCHES' ROCK AT ZENNOR

In the sea off Zennor, near Land's End in Cornwall, the Witches' Rock is still respected for its ability to help. To touch the rock nine times at midnight is regarded as enough to provide insurance against ill-fortune. The rock's association with West Country witches is perhaps more reliable since, according to local comment, it is still used by them for midsummer ritual and celebration.

4 Shape-shifting

Was the werewolf merely a legendary creature, or was he a human who possessed the ability to change to animal form? Did witches escape their hunters by 'shifting their shape' to animal form? Shakespeare may have indicated a knowledge of human shape-shifting abilities when writing in *A Midsummer Night's Dream:*

> *Sometimes a horse I'll be, sometimes a hound,*
> *a hog, a headless boar, sometimes a fire;*
> *And neigh, and bark, and grunt, and roar, and burn,*
> *Like horse, hound, hog, bear, fire, at every turn.*

The lore and the legends not only live on, they are nurtured, nourished and, far from being discarded, they are lived by to this day. Fairy stories from the nursery cradle, childhood rhymes and scholarly scripts, all contain familiar tales which, added to the sayings, beliefs and customs of ages past, can through our folklore, be explored, and explained, but the mystical trail to understanding has been, at times, most carefully concealed.

The ability of a witch to change shape is often recorded, with hares, wolves and dogs being among the most popular alternatives for a witch to shape-shift into from human form. It may only be coincidence but, since so many so-called wild beasts are now often seen on the moors of Devon and Cornwall, the talk of shape-shifting witches has increased.

Dartmoor witches are said to roam the moor in animal (often dog) shape. Black dogs are often the beasts which feature in tales of moorland mysteries. Sometimes the 'beasts' are seen clearly; at other times, they seem no more than a shape in the mists. All have one thing in common: they possess the ability to vanish from sight. Reliable reports are regularly made of 'beasts' seen on moors, some of these mysterious animals having been photographed and filmed. Large dogs, cat-like creatures such as pumas, powerful and prowling, and like their story tale counterparts, displaying one simple ability: they are able to disappear quickly. Despite trained hunters seeking these creatures, the traps stay empty and their identity remains a mystery. Are there even now hunters among the tors prepared with silver shot to save a black witch's soul ?

It has long been believed that witches can transform themselves, or transform others, into a horse. If the witch required a horse to ride, they had only to approach a sleeping victim and place a magic bridle over the sleeper's head to turn them into a mount ready for the road. Shakespeare made much of similar circumstances in *A Midsummer Night's Dream,* and when a performing horse was taken to France during the sixteenth century it was burned as a witch at Rouen, suspected of being the Devil himself!

Even in the UK there are many who still have a fear of the full moon, of the madness it can arouse in humans, the changes it can bring to the normal character, and the shape, of a human.

The fear of lycanthropy (the power of changing oneself into a wolf) continues. The moon-affected wolf-man, the shape-shifting witch, the beliefs of the insane; who will dare to define a difference, and by that definition reveal reality? That most frightening of creatures, the werewolf, is often attributed to East European myth, but the first four letters of the very word itself, taken back to their Latin root *vir* or the Old English *wer* clearly demonstrate one thing - they mean man, not myth. When one of the West Country 'beasts' is eventually caught or killed upon a misty moor, will it provide answers, or add more colour to the curtain drawn between two worlds? Would witches who change their shape at will sacrifice one of their kind to protect the habit of a thousand life-times?

While left to wonder, there are other creatures chosen by shape-shifters to house their souls, that are not at all frightening, and even beautiful, such as swans.

In Devon, the fable continues to be told in the old way. Singers of today, like the balladeers of the past, relate the sad story of the soul of a beautiful maid, returning to her love in the body of a swan, as the result of a tragic accident that took place:

At The Setting Of The Sun

Come all you young fellows that carry a gun,
Beware of late shooting when daylight is done;
For 'tis little you reckon what hazards you run
I shot my true love at the setting of the sun.

In a shower of rain, as my darling did hie,
All under the bushes to keep herself dry,
With her head in her apron, I thought her a swan
And I shot my true love at the setting of the sun.

In the night the fair maid as a white swan appears;
She says, O my true love, quick, dry up your tears,
I freely forgive you, I have paradise won,
I was shot by my true love at the setting of the sun.

Anon

Metempsychosis, the pre-Christian, Celtic belief in the migration of the soul at death, into another body, can be found in a multitude of legends world-wide, and these extend the shape-shifting concept to bridge the gap between the world of the living and the world of the dead.

THE WITCH OF BREWHAM

The woman known as Lydia or Lyda, who inhabited the woods above Brewham, in Somerset, lived there before Alfred's Tower was built. Her name seems not only to be associated with the witches' coven that openly followed the Old Religion in that district, but also with an incident that occurred two centuries and more after the coven, apparently, ceased to practise its rites beneath the trees.

It is far from unusual to hear of women who lived alone referred as 'old hags', or crones, particularly those who selected an isolated spot in which to reside but, with well over two hundred years separating different stories that each definitely identify a Lydia, or Lyda, as the witch of Brewham who lived the woods, there is either evidence here to suggest that the continuity of the ancient craft was being passed on from mothers to daughters who conveniently shared the same name, or that the longevity of just one woman was so exceptional that it perhaps can only be considered as yet another example of witchcraft.

Scientists are already forecasting that the human life-span will soon exceed a hundred and fifty years. Are we discovering a new future, or revisiting forgotten abilities that in previous centuries would have been regarded as being marked by the Devil ? That Lydia was a leading member of the Brewham coven is undoubted, but it is her apparent escape from death more recently that is still spoken of. The Lydia of the nineteenth century who lived in Brewham woods was known as far afield as Glastonbury, Wells and Warminster, where her way with animals made her a woman to consult whenever she was known to be visiting the town.

Farmers and landowners were reluctant to invite the woman into their homes but whenever she set foot upon their property she would be received respectfully and would never leave without the basket she always carried having been filled with food.

The basket was almost Lydia's trademark and in it she would place the birds and small animals she came across on her travels that needed her care and attention. People who knew of her abilities with wildlife brought animals to her, but were never invited into her cottage in the woods; not that many would have dared enter. It always seemed to those who came near the cottage that Lydia suddenly appeared, is if out of nowhere. Almost without exception the people spoke of being aware of the hares that also inhabited the area; or perhaps the one, single hare, that they always saw before Lydia came croaking out of the trees to greet them with a sharp, "What do want?" Hare and woman were never seen together, and some suspected that such an event could never occur, for one obvious reason. The son of a neighbour, who lived no more than three miles from Lydia's cottage, was convinced that Lydia was capable of 'shape-shifting' and that she gained her abilities to treat animals by regularly becoming one of their kind. In the early summer of 1899, the youth was quite convinced that one hare he had often observed repeatedly taking a route from the trees to the meadowland and returning the same way, was indeed the witch of Brewham. One afternoon, carrying his father's shot-gun, he waited in the woods for the hare to return; and it did.

Almost as if following a well-trodden path, the hare scampered up the slope from the meadows towards the shade of the trees. Perhaps the hare heard or saw a movement as the boy took aim because, for some reason, it turned aside as the blast of the gun echoed across the hillside; but the boy was sure he had hit the hare. He tried to convince his father that he had seen it fall but confessed that although he had searched the area thoroughly, there was no sign of the creature he believed he had killed.

There this story might have ended had we not visited a small country fair in the area in 1996. Country crafts were being demonstrated and charcoal burning was being spoken of. Learning of our interest in these matters a local man told us how his grandfather, also a Brewham man, and a charcoal burner, had met a friend in Bruton one day at the close of the old century and had told him how, when he had been on his way home a week or so previously, he had passed Lydia's cottage in the woods and thought he heard her crying out. Without any concern for her reputation as a witch, which he didn't believe anyway, he approached the premises with the intention of offering his help, if help were needed.

His grandfather's knock on the cottage door brought no response but, hearing the cries again, he went to peer in at the window. As his shadow fell across the pane Lydia's voice screeched out, commanding him to leave.

The friend the man's grandfather had been speaking to in Bruton had known the tone of voice his neighbour sometimes used and he was not surprised to learn that the charcoal burner had run off as if the hounds of Hell were after him.

What did surprise him, however, was to be told that in the moment when the man looked through the window and into the cottage he had, without any doubt, seen Lydia removing gun-shot from her shoulder with a darning needle.

5 Witch Ways to Recovery

In the rural areas of the West Country it is not unusual for people to turn away from seeking help for health problems from a doctor and turn instead to a local person who has the reputation for their ability to heal humans and animals alike. Term these people witches if you will, but they exist and thrive today as they have for centuries and we can personally testify to the values and benefits we have enjoyed from encountering men and women who do possess these abilities. While the phrase, 'alternative medicine', has become accepted it is one that conceals reality.

It is only an alternative now to latter-day medication created by a modern industry that has little more than a century of history during which time its calamitous mistakes are usually more readily remembered than its cures.

The wisdom that suggests the use of honey for the treatment of ulcerated legs, is based on its natural ability to heal wounds as recorded in the legends and the history of many countries. It is a wisdom with five thousand years of regular use at least to recommend it.

The witches from Delabole in Cornwall, Tetbury in the Cotswolds, Brewham and Taunton, all shared the same reputation as people who could help and heal and who could be turned to for reliable assistance. In 1807, Matilda of Tetbury is said to have helped a farmworker whose lower leg was nearly severed from his body by the sweep of a scythe. Local people say that the abilities of Matilda were confirmed by the 'miraculous' recovery of the man who was working in the fields again before the crop was collected.

Such a 'miracle' might easily be regarded now as being just an elaboration on the truth but, only a few years ago a countryman we knew was involved in an accident that severed a limb in a similar manner. Only a matter of two weeks or so after hearing of the accident we were surprised to see the man walking towards us, the healing process already complete.

In the area of Delabole there was a witch, Old Annie, who it seems was able to help the afflicted by 'bagging' their troubles and have them take it away themselves in a manner similar to that used by her Brewham counterpart, the witch known there as Lizzie Allen. Both Lizzie and Old Annie followed a similar and specific process.

Whatever troubles ailed the patient, the witch unfolded a piece of cloth and laid it on the ground. In regional variations this cloth is sometimes said to be locally woven in some cases but only simple sacking in others.

The sufferer would stand on the cloth while the witch 'charmed' the illness or disease down their body to the feet, out through the toes and on to the cloth, where it could be wrapped safely to be taken away and buried.

These actions, if we have described them adequately, might be recognised as surprisingly similar to the 'casting out' procedures used by 'spiritual' healers that have become popular in recent years.

The healer, without direct physical contact with the patient, 'pulls and draws' the source of the person's illness down through the body, towards the feet, and ejects it with a final flourish to remove it from within the physical body of the patient.

There are many we know who bear witness that this procedure has brought relief to a sufferer. None would consider that the remedy was associated with the ancient craft of the witch.

Old Annie, we learned from a friend in Boscastle, was said to have the ability to help people from a distance, without personal contact. The Rev Baring Gould similarly relates how a witch of his acquaintance, Anne Abell, who died in 1881 aged 82 years, had helped a severely injured man without being anywhere near him.

Rather like Old Annie, the witch from Delabole, Anne Abell was once called upon to help a farmer who had severely slashed his leg with a scythe. Unable to get to the witch, the man remained where he had fallen while his handkerchief, soaked with his blood, was taken to her and the farmer carried to his home. The carrier of the bloodstained cloth and the carriers of the bloodsoaked man all recalled that it was an hour after noon when they reached their respective destinations.

Anne Abell took the cloth and blessed it with a sealing spell.

At about that same time, in their home, the farmer's wife was preparing to clean her husband's wound but, to her amazement, she found that the blood had ceased to flow and that the enormous gash was sealing, seemingly of its own accord.

The Rev Baring Gould had good cause to know Anne Abell, as she was his tenant. He wrote that he firmly believed the powers she possessed were powers that she used regularly when providing help to others.

How the wound was healed from a distance remains a mystery. It is said that 'faith' can achieve all things, but witches are said to know many ways to staunch the flow of blood.

OF COBWEBS AND PERIWINKLE

The use of cobwebs, applied by a witch to wounds to stop them bleeding, is widely regarded to be a very ancient cure. It was witchcraft regularly recalled for us by people who live in town, as well as by country dwellers. The general belief being that blood adheres to the strands of web, inducing coagulation and causing a scab to form.

However, while many instances of the use of this method of healing can be found, no one suggested that frantic farmworkers, having scythed a leg in a meadow miles from home, or carpenters cutting their thighs to the bone, were likely to have gone off collecting cobwebs afterwards!

The many similar incidents recorded all confirm that the life of the injured party was preserved by the one person who could heal wounds quickly when called upon: the local witch. When discussing these matters with elderly West Country folk, it is always the local woman, or man, who possessed such knowledge that they themselves remembered or that they had heard their parents speak of. In rural areas or in towns, the local witch who used things that were easily and readily available to them when an emergency arose was valued in the community; even if feared.

Only the title 'witch' seems to have been dropped today. In most cases when the local herbalist is referred to, it is the knowledge and abilities they possess which appear to be exactly like those known to Matilda, Annie or Lizzie, all of whom were witches of high repute. Theirs was a knowledge from which periwinkle gained the name 'cut-finger'.

Periwinkle's special medicinal values as a binder speedily stemmed the flow of blood, and its nickname remains as a reminder of natural means, non-drug induced, of blood coagulation available for centuries to West Country witches; and they still use it when necessary, to remedy the troubles its name clearly defines.

'PETER'S STONE'

The evidence can still be seen on some West Country religious buildings, of damage done to them by people intent on pursuing remedies that, mysteriously, did work.

Stone taken from statuettes of saints, removed from church and ground down to powder, was often recorded as providing the basic ingredient for a cure against ills or bewitchment imposed by witchcraft.

Henderson's *Folk-Lore of the Northern Counties*, 1879, provides an example of 'Peter's Stone' being used to treat the breast problems suffered by a lady in Devon who attributed her troubles to a local witch. After her baby was born the woman found that she was unable to breast-feed the child, and that any attempt to do so was painful. Her husband walked by night from Teignmouth to Exeter Cathedral with but one intention; to steal some sacred stone. In the middle of the night, by the light of the moon, the man flung objects against the sculpted figures on the west front of the Cathedral, sometimes called St Peter's, until he succeeded in breaking an arm off one figure.

Seizing the precious stone, the man hastened home in triumph to his ailing wife and there he pulverized his prize, mixed it with herbs and fats and applied it to his wife's breast to bring her relief and comfort from her pains.

LOST LIMBS

A very close relative seldom spoke of his experiences in the First World War, but childhood memories were revived when we found ourselves listening to a man of fifty who spoke of lost limbs. Our relative had endured the Great War along with many other West Countrymen but also, like them, lost many friends during the conflict. His memories of them never dimmed, nor of the final service he and others provided for some who fell. During a lull in battle, whenever there was an opportunity, the bodies of fallen comrades were recovered from the battlefield. The entire body, if at all possible. "We wanted to bury our pals properly," was what he had said. "Collect the pieces and give them a proper burial, all together. We had to do it. That was the way it was."

Nearly fifty years later those comments, made to a wide-eyed kid by a soldier made old by war, were remembered when we learned that it was once a custom, recorded in the West Country, that limbs lost through accident should be preserved and safely retained until the owner died and their complete body could be buried.

It was done to protect the owner of the lost limb against a witch taking possession of their unsuspecting soul soon after it started its journey from the body after death. The lost limb would be kept in a safe and secret place until it could be 'restored' to its owner.

Between the two World Wars the custom of keeping a workman's finger, cut from his hand by a chaffing machine, was noted to have occurred in the county of Devon.

In 1949, half an inch of a young boy's little finger was sewn back on. Before the procedure, his parents had asked the doctors for the tip to be kept, for later burial, if the attempt at restoration was not successful. We know without doubt that the operation succeeded.

When medical treatment was not so readily available, the assistance of the local witch continued to be called upon for the treatment of ills and ailments, and she also acted as midwife.

The coffin cure was recommended for the treatment of boils by the witches of Crediton, not long ago; it calls for the offending boils to be poulticed for three days and three nights. Sufferers were advised to retain each pus-filled poultice as it is replaced with a fresh one and at the end of the treatment time to place the poultices, accompanied with all cloth used to bind them around the boils, in the coffin of a recently deceased person who is about to be buried.

Bury the poultices with the body, and the boils would be banished, never to return.

Not a remedy readily followed today perhaps, but many of the country cures originally concocted by wise women, or witches, do still find favour, naturally.

6 Gypsy Witchcraft

Gypsies have endured their reputation for practising witchcraft since they first arrived in England in the early sixteenth century and found that the beauty and wilderness of the Forest of Dean, in Gloucestershire, was an attractive location to return to after roaming the country. By calling themselves 'Dukes (or Lords) of Little Egypt' they created a name that became both honoured and feared.

Originating in India, as the true gypsy tribes drifted westward they were attributed with being descendants of the first murderer, Cain, accused of making the nails used in Christ's crucifixion, of deceiving people with palmistry, and possessing the magical powers of witchcraft.

The great profession of the real gypsies still is the telling of fortunes (dukkerin' drey the vast) from the lines in the hand, or by the turn of the cards.

During the reign of Henry VIII, gypsies were considered to be vagabonds who ought to serve a master in one definite locality, but who preferred to wander about the country in search of adventure. They were considered obnoxious people, not because of their witchcraft but because they went from shire to shire. They managed to upset the Old Church and the New by insisting that none of their tribe should be buried in consecrated ground. Then, and during the centuries that followed, to be buried outside God's blessed acre was a fate reserved for suicides, criminals and the like, and any whose souls were to be condemned.

In 1530 it became a criminal offence merely to be a gypsy and from that time onwards, until 1784 when the laws were changed, many were to suffer execution. Belief in the supernatural occupied a vital role in gypsy communities. Others who learned of their belief that evil spirits roamed the night, seeking victims, and that gypsies collected small holed stones, the breastbones of kingfishers or jays, and looked for four-leaved clover, all considered that these items were prized for their witchcraft values; while the gypsies carried them as lucky charms.

The gypsies of Philip and Mary's time were declared felons if they would not depart a place within 40 days but, if they left their "naughty, idle, and ungodly life and company and be placed in the service of some honest and able inhabitant within the realm, or exercise some lawful calling, they were to be discharged of all the pains and forfeitures contained in the Act".

As the earliest of 'witches' the gypsy women were feared for their ability to cast the Evil Eye on anyone who upset them.

To be stared at by a gypsy was enough to ensure bewitchment, if not death.

Elizabeth I made it a felony to be seen in any company or fellowship of vagabonds calling themselves 'Egyptians' and this was considered so important that records of prosecution were preserved in the secret bag of the King's Bench. Four yeomen from Medmensham, in Buckinghamshire, were accused of feloniously keeping company with a band of gipsies and of "counterfeiting, transforming, and altering themselves in dress, language, and behaviour to such vagabonds called Egyptians". They were found guilty and sentenced to be hanged.

THE DEVIL'S INSTRUMENT

Surprisingly, to us at least, we can both remember, in our early years, sitting in gypsy camps, enjoying the company of true gypsies, eating with them, and learning from them. Every summer we awaited their return, one by the Severn, the other by the Thames, and over half a century later the music we danced to with our friends remains clear to our ears.

The stories they told us we now find we shared since we both knew the story of why the Devil made the violin. The instrument did not exist when a gypsy girl, Mara, fell in love with a young gorgio (a non gypsy) who, despite her beauty, took no notice of her at all. Mara tried all ways to attract him when he came to their atchin-tan (camp) to bargain for horses with her father, who brought such livestock from one shire to another as they travelled the country.

Her cooking pleased him, her parent's vardo (living wagon) intrigued him, but as for Mara, he ignored her. In despair, Mara called on o Bengh (the Devil) to help her. o Bengh agreed to attract the gorgio to her - on one condition - that she sold her family's souls to him in exchange for this service.

She, instead, offered him her own soul, her grai, and her jukel (horse and dog), but when these were scorned, torn between love for her family and love for her man, she reluctantly agreed to o Bengh's proposition.

The pact agreed, o Bengh plucked up her father and from him formed the sound-box of a new musical instrument. From Mara's five brothers he fashioned four strings and a bridge, and from her mother, he made a bow. From seven souls sold to him o Bengh created an instrument that possessed magical qualities capable of captivating for their lifetime all who heard it. He taught the beautiful gypsy girl to play the wonderful instrument and, when the gorgio saw her and heard her playing, he fell in love, and his heart was hers.

Their lives together were long, happy and rewarding, until o Bengh returned to claim Mara's soul, and that of her husband too; for she had agreed to sell all the souls in her family, and that, o Bengh said, included theirs.

As the gypsy couple were carried off to Hell, the violin fell to the ground. It lay among some rocks, until it was found one day by a poor gypsy boy who let the magic of Mara's music be heard again and, since that time, the gypsy and the violin have been as one.

Among gypsies, strands of the Old Religion appear more frequently and naturally in everyday life than, perhaps, they appear in our lives.

The profession of tribal chovihani (witch) is passed down from mother to daughter and the knowledge and understanding of plants, shrubs, flowers, and trees, and their individual true values is similarly handed down by the drabarni (herb woman) who, when absorbed in the work of producing natural medicines, peering into a cauldron that was suspended over an open fire, would easily provide any casual observer with the impression that they had witnessed a witch at work.

If we, as children of the 1940s had been seen by some city salesman who passed by on a summer night, while we were dancing wildly around a campfire with our gypsy friends, to music played on a violin, as the evening meal was being prepared in a cauldron on the open fire, the talk of the town next day would have been of witchcraft, witnessed beyond doubt. The salesman would probably not have paid for another pint of beer for years as he told and retold the tale of the witches' Sabbat he had seen, and by Christmas would probably have been recounting the tale as one of a Sabbat he had escaped from.

Roughly translated, the gypsy proverb, *Ki shan i Romani, Adoi san' i chov'han*, states that "where the Romanies go, so will the witches be found" and throughout their history the gypsies have been considered among the foremost practitioners of witchcraft wherever their tribes have wandered. The Romany belief in the Amari De, the Great Mother, or De Develeski, the personification of Nature, represented more often today by Sara-Kali, the Black Madonna, continues to be beyond the understanding of those who follow the many religions of the gorgios.

Much like those of the Jewish faith, the true gypsies prefer their young to marry within the tribe and we recall from our childhood that the half-breeds, whom the gypsies referred to as Diddikais, were not welcomed in our country area in anywhere near the same way as our gypsy friends.

They talked to us quite openly and naturally of reincarnation, the phases of the moon, nature, the gods and goddesses and, before our minds could become fettered, provided us with enough advice to keep our minds open; and perhaps that is the touch of gypsy witchcraft that really matters.

7 Curses and Spells

The witch's curse can be found in tales and legends related in every country. The eye of a toad and leg of a newt, or similar ingredients, added to the unfathomable concoction being boiled up in a cauldron, are stock-in-trade curse components. Whatever ancient beliefs lie behind the stories of Sleeping Beauty and the enchanted spindle of her spinning wheel that was used to induce her death-like sleep, or of Snow White's temptation, when the offer of a rosy-red evil apple might end in misery, these stories remain popular; and are regularly told.

In Somerset, a curse can come in other ways. In 1886 an old house in Wellington was being renovated, and a secret room was discovered in the space between a bedroom and the roof by workmen. Six broomsticks found in the hidden room, a seat, and other, more unusual objects, convinced the finders that they had discovered a witches' meeting place.

One curious find defied explanation. It was a three-strand rope, five feet long, half an inch thick, looped at one end, and with goose, and crow or rook feathers stuck right through the rope-strands at irregular intervals. The object was observed with alarm by some older Somerset people, who declined to touch it.

The workmen called the object a 'witches' ladder', but it was later identified as being something used to lay a curse on someone, or something. Further information led us to believe that, when it was first made, the rope would have been new and the feathers taken from a male bird. This system of placing a curse was known in other parts of the West Country, and also in Italy as *La guirlande delle streghe,* the witches' garland, where black hen's feathers were tied into the rope in knots.

The curse to be applied was repeated continually as the feathers were put into place, and when the charm was completed it would be hidden in the bed of the person to be cursed to bring misfortune upon them swiftly.

In his novel, *Curgenven,* published in 1893, the Rev Baring-Gould introduced the curse of the witches' ladder into the plot, demonstrating his personal knowledge of witchcraft. The ladder he describes in detail was made of black wool entwined with brown and white thread. Every two inches, this cord was tied round a bunch of cock's, pheasant's, or moorhen's feathers, set alternately. Into each knot the maker wove the curse that all kinds of aches and pains should be suffered by her intended victim.

The finished curse was taken by her to Dozmary Pool on Bodmin Moor and cast into the water. As the ladder sank, and bubbles rose to the top of the pool, the curse was believed to be working.

The knotted rope appears again in spells found in the West Country. Brewing up a storm, and selling the wind, were two popular spells that could be purchased or obtained from witches in Cornwall and Devon. Sir Francis Drake is reputed to have consorted with Plymouth witches and to have received from them the winds that blew the ships of the Spanish Armada to their destruction. Sailors leaving these shores would similarly, and equally willingly, frequent with witches in order to obtain from them the winds that could be released whenever their ship was becalmed, or their lives endangered. These winds were safely, for the time being, contained in knots tied into a length of three-stranded rope, knots that had been tied with a purpose. The rope, some say, had been used by the witches who suspended their cauldron, off the coast, above the boiling seas as they 'brewed up a storm', and into each knot they had sealed the eye of a storm. The use of the magical number three appears three times in the spell; the strands of rope, the eyes of three storms, three knots each providing the promise of success.

The perfect trinity, perhaps.

RICHARD III

Richard III arrived in Exeter during November 1483, but his coming was not bloodless, although the Mayor welcomed him with all "solemnity and outward joy".

A E Freeman, a nineteenth-century historian, writes of the hump-back that, when the King heard the name Rougemont, he was in the words of an all but contemporary writer "suddenly fallen into a great dump, and as it were a man amazed".

Shakespeare provides a more poetic version and permits Richard to deliver these lines:

Richmond! When I was last at Exeter,
The mayor in courtesy showed me the castle,
And called it Rougemont - at which name I started;
Because a bard of Ireland told me once,
I should not live long after I saw Richmond.

The forecast was correct. Richard didn't live long after seeing Rougemont Castle and died very soon after seeing Richmond, its Earl.

JOHN WESLEY

While travelling through and preaching the Gospel in Cornwall during the eighteenth century, John Wesley recorded an incident in his journal, on 13 August 1746, of an encounter that he experienced with a curse.

After Wesley had delivered his sermon, an old woman waited until the crowd around him dispersed before coming forward to thank him, and to tell him that his words that day had provided her with respite and ease from arthritis or rheumatism; or those were the ailments he thought she had mentioned. Her reason for thanking him, it seems, was because some seven years earlier, a woman she had upset for some reason had gone to a wizard and paid him a fee to put a curse on her.

Wesley had been intrigued by her comments and later noted that she had told him she had known exactly when it was that the wizard had bewitched her. Apparently there had been a sudden storm that woke her in her bed and while she hid herself under the covers, away from the thunder and lightning, she had felt her flesh burn and she knew that the Devil was attacking her. From that time onwards not a day had passed without her feeling her body in torment, as if her flesh were being torn from it, piece after piece, by burning pincers.

Every day her mind had been crowded with fear and horror as the curse continued and she waited for the Devil to return. Not by day nor by night had she rested; not until she had heard the words uttered by him. Her mind was at rest and she was convinced that Wesley had, by his presence and his words, removed the wizard's curse.

THE BLOWING CURSE
We were reminded of the simple everyday fear that people held of witches while visiting Holsworthy, in Devon, where we learned that witches there had been known to blow lice on to people they wished to infect. Relief from the curse could only be achieved by telling others of the affliction and passing the problem on to them. While some women, we were advised, did hold the powers to recognise a witch, and could advise others to avoid them, these same women were apparently powerless when it came to protecting their own families.

The hygiene standards of past ages were low indeed, and the spread of disease, or even lice, was common enough but not understood, which probably explains the belief that witches could harm others with their lice-spreading spells. Though this doesn't explain why, in our conversations, the 'blowing curse' was said to have been the cause of a recent outbreak of head-lice among school children.

POPPETS, PUPPETS AND MOMMETS
It is, perhaps, the image-magic of witchcraft that is most widely known and feared. The fear that evil can be cast upon a person, through a 'doll' made in their likeness, is a fear that is known world-wide.

Poppets, mommets or puppets are all doll-like reproductions of a person, and have long been associated with witchcraft, both black and white, in the West Country. Elaborate and thought-provoking examples of these dolls can be seen in the Museum of Witchcraft in Boscastle, Devon. 'Hold your tongue' might even now be a command to be obeyed, by some, when the voice of authority is heard but a poppet in which an appropriately placed pin ensures that the command becomes a curse that cannot be evaded is something far more sinister to encounter.

Beliefs expressed in the fifteenth century still linger on. Then it was said, by witches of the western counties, that illness or death could be caused by making a likeness of a person, in clay, and pricking the image with pins.

In *The Return of The Native* (1878), Thomas Hardy provides a graphic description of the image-making, pin-pricking practices employed by Susan Nunsuch when she fears that an evil spell has been put upon her son by Eustacia Yeobright. Such figures are still being found, and used, in the twentieth century.

A doll, formed in the figure of US President McKinley was riddled with pins and burnt on the steps of the American Embassy in London. The clay-formed likeness of a naked woman, its 'heart' penetrated through with a sliver of hawthorn, has more recently been found; its obvious intention was to kill.

The need for protection from spells is not restricted.

In Devon there are ghostly beasts reputed to be guarding churches and churchyards from the undesirable attention of witches, or worse.

In the parish of Lew Trenchard, according to the Rev Baring Gould, the guardians are said to be two white pigs yoked together with a silver chain. In an adjoining parish it is a black dog that is claimed to be in spiritual residence and, in yet another rural parish, it is said to be a calf that acts as protector to the church.

THE BIRDLIP CURSE

Those who know the road from Gloucester to Cirencester will know Birdlip where a hill of some notoriety still presents dangers to travellers even in this modern age. Over two centuries ago, horse drawn carts used what was then little more than a rutted rock-strewn track that carriers could follow only with difficulty at the best of times to get to the Cotswold town and nearby villages. From one of those villages came twin sisters - girls who were as different as chalk and cheese - and while one grew up to marry a carter who struggled for his living, the other married into a wealthy farming family. Fate, if that was all it was, first stepped into the girls' lives when they chose husbands whose surnames were the same, though the men were not related. It is a family name still widely recognised in the county so, exercising discretion, and quite adequately for our purposes, we shall simply refer to the family as 'Weaver', with apologies to all other families who share that respectable name.

The wife of wealthy farmer Jacob Weaver had aspirations to rise in society and was, quite unreasonably, jealous of her sister, the wife of a carter, Elias Weaver. Elias worked hard and long to make a living, and his wife toiled at his side. She was a woman whose strength he often relied upon and he missed her help on those five occasions when childbirth kept her away from his side for a few short weeks in each of five successive years.

The farmer's family similarly increased during those years but, instead of his wife sharing the joy of motherhood with her sister, her jealousy increased and she continually ill-wished the carter, his wife and their family. In the comfort of her home she sat for hours on end vainly attempting to bring misfortune down upon the heads of her sister and her family; and became ever more frustrated when she failed. There was no two-way traffic in these evil actions, as the carters had long since decided to ignore their wealthy relations and went out of their way to avoid conflict.

On Birdlip hill one day, their best of intentions failed them when, as they were homeward bound from Gloucester market, they encountered the farming family going in the opposite direction, riding matching greys. With the cart taking up most of the road and its team struggling up the hill the horses of the approaching riders were forced to give way. Perhaps that trifling incident triggered the troubles that followed.

That night the farmer's wife forced her husband to seek out a witch who was known in Gloucester. She instructed him to pay the witch to place a curse on the carter's family and seal the success of the curse by burying a bull's heart, pricked with pins, in the pathway to their home. The witch agreed that the curse could be laid on the night of the full moon, some eight nights later, and the farmer hurried back to confirm the witch's agreement to his wife, who could hardly wait for the time to pass and who spent sleepless nights wondering what form her sister's downfall would take. On the fateful day, by some pretext or another, she contrived to be in Cirencester by mid-morning, in reality hoping to hear tell of what had befallen her sister. No such news became apparent; on the contrary, the villagers seemed to expect her to be pleased to hear that her brother-in-law's cartage business was booming.

She barely hid her displeasure, returned to the farm in a violent temper, where she collapsed and was taken to her bed. The doctor was summoned and, while providing medication in return for his attendance fee, he later commented to colleagues that he diagnosed strong liquor as being the likely cause of the lady's misfortune. Such private comments, seemingly uttered in safe surroundings, somehow soon became county-wide conversation.

To save his wife being condemned by ribald remarks regarding her consumption of unsuitable spirits, the farmer once more sought out the witch, who, surprised by the situation, promised to help. It was nightfall by the time the farmer arrived home from Gloucester and as he strode towards his door in the the darkness he came across a stooping figure. He wrestled with the intruder, bringing the figure close to the door as a servant hurried out to assist him. Candlelight from the hallway fell across the face of the witch, and on to the pin-pricked heart she was trying to conceal in her cloak.

The truth could not remain hidden. The witch confessed that she had not known the name of the farmer who had called upon her to cast her spell, and admitted that when she came to lay down the curse, not knowing the area well, she had asked villagers to direct her to the Weaver household.

That she had been directed to the wrong sister's abode, became apparent only when the farmer had given her his account of what had happened to his wife.

That the farmer's wife died, their crops failed, and their children perished at an early age, is a matter of family history.

The business of the Cotswold carter flourished and his descendants still climb Birdlip hill unhindered by a witch who made one simple mistake; unless, as they believe, a greater force intervened.

MISSING PERSONS

Many legends, traditions and tales recorded by chroniclers, poets and authors tell of potions obtained from witches that will ensure the return of a straying lover, or the 'capture' of a new love. In July 1889, extracts from business correspondence received the previous October by Mr J J Ogilvie Evans of Teignmouth were included in a report to the Devonshire Association. The extracts, and his comments, reveal methods still then being sought for such success,

A lady wrote to ask if Mr Ogilvie Evans knew whether such a thing as 'Oil of Man' was available. He replied, saying that it was no longer available. Later he received a further letter which advised him that the lady's husband had left her some months earlier and that she had been advised to burn the elusive 'Oil of Man' to ensure his return.

The lady would welcome advice on any alternative substance that might be available and could be recommended.

While the contents of any possible further correspondence with the lady were not recorded, Mr Ogilvie Evans did explain to the Association the earlier uses for 'Oil of Man'. It had, he stated, been used for centuries; in his *Royal Pharmacopoeia*, 1678, Moses Charras directs it to be made by distillation of the skulls of healthy men who have been recently hanged, or who otherwise met with a violent death.

In the sixteenth century, W Salmon, at his house, the 'Blew Bul", in Shoe Lane, London, where he pursued the art and mystery of an apothecary "through the assistance of Divine Help", prepared and sold *Potestates craniivhumani* at 10/- (50p) an ounce (approx 50g).

The Association report then notes that "a correspondent says that in his early days *Oleum humanum* was boiled out of the bones of dissected subjects by the hospital porter, and was in great request".

In conclusion, Mr Ogilvie Evans confirms the lady's request for a potion to bring someone back not to be an isolated one. Belief in the magical powers of drugs was, and in many ways still is, widespread in Britain. He knew of a chemist in Cranleigh, Essex, who was asked to supply an oil which, if a few drops were placed on a letter, would ensure a reply being received and even possibly result in the return of the person to whom it was addressed; in this instance an errant daughter.

Another chemist he knew received the following request: "Please sir, I want some powder - I don't know its name, but it is salmon-coloured - for a neighbour. She wants to burn it in the fire to fetch her husband back from

America. My husband left me a short time ago, so I burnt some of the powder and it brought him back."

ILL-WISHING EVIL EYES

The ability to overpower a victim simply by 'looking' at them, was, and is, considered to be one of a witch's most evil powers.

A century ago, the wife of a farm labourer from the Ashburton area became depressed and it was thought that she would harm herself, or even take her own life. An application was made to have her certified insane and committed to an asylum. The magistrate visited her in May 1893 and she told him that her husband was responsible for her condition. She said that her husband and neighbours had come up behind her when she was looking in a mirror and their reflections had 'overshadowed' hers in the glass. Thereby they had taken away her power of will and by doing so they became answerable for her actions.

Witches or otherwise, anyone who possessed the 'evil eye' was someone to be feared. The malevolent power resided in 'identifiable' people, especially those with squint eyes; and those with eyes of an unusual hue; and not forgetting those who possessed a penetrating gaze.

With nothing more than a silent stare they could cause a cow to go dry, or die; hooded eyes half hidden could flash and cause crops to fail, accidents to occur, misfortune to mar many a man's future - male virility was considered to be especially vulnerable - and, worse still, perhaps, they could threaten the very salvation of a soul; man, woman or child. Unbelievable? Perhaps. But how often is the phrase, "if looks could kill", still heard nowadays?

On her way to the gallows at Heavitree, Exeter, to be executed in 1862, having been found guilty of the crime of witchcraft, Susanna Edwardes was said have cast her evil eye on one of her escort guards, whereupon the man began to foam at the mouth, leaped about wildly like a madman, and finally collapsed in the street and died.

Amulets and talismans were made and sought after to protect people and animals from such attack by a person having the 'evil eye'. Horse brasses were originally designed and introduced for the purpose of protection, with similar amulets developed for other animals while for humans, amulets taking the form of an erect phallus would be worn.

If a man felt himself threatened, a sign made with the hand could ward off the immediate evil; he thrust his thumb between the first and second fingers of his hand to symbolise the penis penetrating the vulva.

For more effective protection, particularly where babies were concerned, holy water, much like saintly stone, was considered to hold values that were more precious than gold. Sprinkled around a cradle the water would avert the evil eye, ward off evil and prevent a child from being 'overlooked'.

In the past, fonts were often kept locked to prevent the holy water being stolen. The fears of being cursed by the evil eye, or beset by troubles through ill-wishing, are certainly not fears that have disappeared. Phrases like, 'if looks could kill,' or, 'you've only got to look at her/him,' or 'look what you've made me do,' crop up in normal conversation today in towns, cities, villages, and hamlets everywhere; and when they are spoken they express, however unwittingly, the fears or the understanding of centuries of evil eye and ill-wishing practices.

There are volumes of material written today on the power of thought, or the power of positive thinking, and a multitude of similar 'creative' methods of control that can be used in business or life in general to attain success. Business organisations pay hundreds of thousands of pounds to individuals who claim that they are capable of inspiring and teaching salespeople and executives how to influence their customers or clients by using mind-bending techniques that will ensure they achieve their goal. How far then have we progressed since bewitching, cursing, ill-wishing, over looking, or putting a spell on someone, were enough to bring down accusations that witchcraft was at work?

A man in Shaftesbury once thought that he had been 'overlooked' by his sister-in-law who didn't want him to succeed in life. He was unable to work, as his doctor confirmed, but neither the medical man nor the patient could give a reason for his affliction. The man, if not the doctor, recognised that witchcraft was the cause of his problems. His wife went to a 'wise woman' in Stalybridge for help and her powers are said to have helped relieve the problem for a short time, but the man succumbed again to what he and his wife by then totally believed was ill-wishing by some person or other. The man, unable to work, was eventually forced to apply for relief - financial help - from the Shaftesbury Union.

Little more than a century ago, in 1884, the *Bridport News* carried items concerning a case of 'overlooking.' The wife of a woodsman, who lived near Dorchester, had been ill for some time and unable to find a medical practitioner capable of relieving her sickness, or at times even unable to diagnose her symptoms. In her continuing distress she consulted a gypsy, who told her that she had obviously been 'over looked', and was afflicted by unnatural powers.

The woman's distress increased when the gypsy warned her that she would not recover until the spell was broken, but eased a little when the gypsy offered, for a fee, to attempt to break the spell. The desperate invalid readily agreed to the suggestion, pleased that someone was, at last, prepared to help her.

At the direction of her Romany friend, the woman collected together some personal possessions and some pot-plants and placed them, all together, out of doors. She was promised by the gypsy that when the flowers withered and died, so her affliction would also wither away, and depart her body, and her recovery would commence. At this point, while reading the newspaper accounts, it was easy for anyone to dismiss the woman as being gullible, the gypsy as being an opportunist, and the fee as being a fool's payment, until reaching the concluding comments in the report.

The instructions it seems were followed implicitly and as the flowers withered away the woman's illness diminished and by the time the flowers had died she had made a full recovery.

The continued acceptance of witchcraft in the West Country found favour with newspaper editors who regularly included both news items and correspondence on the craft.

A letter appeared in the *Western Morning News* on 9 February 1928 in which the writer stated that:

> *I am informed by reliable people in this neighbourhood that about fifty or so years ago a number of persons from East Cornwall were in the habit of visiting a celebrated witch in Plymouth for help and advice in cases of ill wishing &c., and the two following examples from this district have been related to me.*
>
> *A farmer having had his farm-stock ill-wished, visited the aforesaid witch and was told to take the heart of one of the animals which had met with a mysterious death, stick it full of pins and burn it with fire in the centre of one his fields at midnight, at the same time uttering some strange words the witch gave him. This he did, and the spell was immediately removed.*
>
> *To another man the witch produced in some mysterious way a photograph of the person who had ill-wished him and he was requested to strike the unfortunate female whom it happened to portray on any part of her body but not with the intent to kill.*
>
> *He struck the portrait of the ill-wisher across the leg, and was told, after paying the usual fee, that on his homeward journey he would find her lying by the roadside with her leg broken. Sure enough he did, and the spell was at once removed, or, at least, it was said he suffered no further losses.*

The individual to whom these troubled people turned between the wars was apparently known as the White Witch of Plymouth.

A SPECIAL CHARM TO PRESERVE CATTLE FROM WITCHCRAFT

Reginald Scot, in his *Discoverie of Witchcraft* (1584 refers to the charm that was used both in the West Country and the Highlands of Scotland.

> *At Easter you must take certain drops that lie uppermost of the holy paschal candle, and make a little wax candle thereof; and upon some Sunday morning light and hold it so as it may drop upon and between the horns and ears of the beast, saying, In nomine Patris et Filii, &c., and burn the beast a little between the horns on the ears with the same wax, and that which is left thereof stick it cross-wise about the stable or stall, or upon the threshold, or over the door, where the cattle use to go in and out; and for all that year your cattle shall never be bewitched.*

PORTRAIT OF THE ARTIST AS . . .

St Ives in Cornwall has assumed the mantle of being the West Country's leading centre for the arts over the past hundred years but long before it became fashionable for the less talented, but wealthy, to identify groups of artists as 'schools' for ease of recognition, the south-west peninsula with its light, scenery and, more particularly, its pre-Christian Celtic connections and influences, has provided artistic inspiration. Art, in its most influential form, had been presented to the people through their churches since religion first came to these islands and the remains of this communication through art is still being found on the walls of some of the older churches in the south-west.

In 1885 a young hard-working artist was encouraged by the Rev Sabine Baring-Gould, for four years the rector of Lew Trenchard in West Devon, to leave London and to come westward for a time. Members of Baring Gould's family were artistic and their interest in the artist was perhaps influenced by the young man's knowledge of church screen paintings which, like the earliest church work, relates the Christian stories in a pictorial form. The family's work remains to be seen to this day on the screens in Lew Trenchard church.

The family's artist friend settled in rented accommodation near St Ives and was completing his first painting in these new surroundings when he was startled by a visitor who, surprisingly, addressed him by name. Turning away from his work, a portrait, he faced an elderly man who came striding towards him, hand outstretched in greeting. He later told his London friends that for some reason he ignored the gesture but enquired the man's name and business in a cordial manner.

Uninvited, the man removed his long coat and sat at ease as he told the artist that he too was an painter and had, at one time, also used these premises. Not wishing to appear inhospitable the artist tried to continue his work while holding a conversation with the visitor who, apparently, did not share his interest in religious paintings. He recalled being concerned when the man's manner seemed to alter when the artist tried to bring the conversation to a close.

To the artist's horror, instead of leaving, the man pushed him aside, seized a brush and added a few strokes to the painting on the easel. Replacing the brush the stranger held out his hand again, but again it was ignored, rather more pointedly this time. The man just laughed as he picked up his coat and made the comment, "You will find that my addition to your work will ensure that it is remembered, though you never will be, unless you accept my help. Come, let us shake hands on the pact."

The artist ignored the extended hand of friendship for the third time. He gritted his teeth, not allowing the offensive and impudent remark to rile him, and insisted that his unwelcome visitor leave.

Later, when visiting a local inn, he asked others there if they could identify the arrogant intruder. His question was greeted by silent stares, before some turned their backs to him. A few drank up and left hurriedly. As silence descended the landlord nodded towards the end of the bar and made his way there. The artist followed and, ignored by everyone in the room, listened carefully to what the landlord had to say. He learned that the previous tenant had also experienced a similar encounter, but that he had shaken the visitor by the hand. The man had related that the visitor's grip was a savage one,and that when their hands were clasped, the stranger, using his free hand, slashed deep marks on the back of his hand.

"He came in here to show us the cuts," the landlord commented as he pulled the artist another pint. "Told 'em it was worse than shaking hands with the devil." He placed the brimming glass on the bar and leaned forward. "Those marks were still there," he added, "when they cut his body down from the beam in your cottage, where he hanged himself a few weeks later. There was no doubt for any of us - he had shaken hands with the Devil." The artist noted the knowing nods and winks exchanged between locals at the conclusion of the tale, which he dismissed as one told to fool visitors such as himself, from 'Lunnun'.

He dismissed the tale until a few days later, when he decided to finish the portrait he had been working on: his self-portrait.

But the picture that he found on his easel was not of his fresh-faced self, but that of an older version of his person, the jaw unshaven, the forehead lined.

His response was immediate; he destroyed the canvas and returned to London. Back in the city he soon felt at ease mixing and mingling with his artist and writer friends, some of whom gained fame, and who ensured his story was remembered long after he was forgotten.

Oscar Wilde was a leading figure in the literary set at the time, and the artist's experiences intrigued him. There is no record of the young artist ever achieving success in his field, but the story that Wilde published in 1891, *The Picture of Dorian Gray*, a tale that contrasts totally with Wilde's brilliantly witty comedies, is perhaps a story that shows what the artist might have achieved, had he sealed his pact with the stranger, and shaken hands with the Devil himself.

8 Witch Lore

Think of a witch, her cottage, cauldron, and assorted paraphernalia, and the picture conjured up in the mind will usually include the witch's cat. Cats, especially black ones, have always been associated with the supernatural, although the cat in *Macbeth* was 'brindled', and the word 'grimalken', meaning 'old grey cat', was often applied contemptuously in the West Country to some old women in past centuries.

Feared as the familiars of the witches in this kingdom, cats were sacred beasts in Egypt. The cat goddess Bast appears to have been a feline form of Isis. In the sacred city of Bubastis, and other places in Egypt, the carefully mummified bodies of cats have been found. In carefully concealed places in the West Country, the mummified remains of cats have been also been found. The Devil is sometimes said to appear at Sabbats in the form of a cat. The moon Goddess Diana sometimes similarly chooses to appear in feline form to her followers. Pan, the horned god, appears as a goat; the cat and the goat are the animals most associated with witchcraft. Were the pagan Gods of our ancestors similarly seen, and is this fixation with cats a reminder of something once held sacred, in an Old Religion?

The much abused and rarely understood word 'pagan' (someone who is neither Christian, Jewish nor Muslim, ie a heathen) is conveniently used by western religious leaders to confuse the issue of earlier Gods and older religions but the cult of the cat continues to find favour in many homes in the modern world.

Never mind the witches, cats have themselves been attributed with many predictive powers that are now regarded as a harmless part of folklore, but could once have cost a woman her life:

If a cat, seen cleaning itself, puts its paws over both ears, then a stranger can be expected to arrive soon.
If it washes only its face, a friend is on their way to pay you a visit.
If it washes above its ears, it is going to rain.
When a cat is washing its ears, the first person it looks up at will receive a letter.
A cat curled on a chair, the top of its head downwards against a cushion, asleep on its back, would be seen as predicting rain.
"If a cat sleeps on her brain, it's a sure sign of rain."
A sneezing cat is a sign of heavy rain coming in and, if one is seen to be scratching itself, it is said to be "bringing down the rain", virtually encouraging it.
The cat which can probably be relied upon to be "right more times than wrong", is the one that sneaks into the house, and sits with its back to the fire. This is that cat that is expecting a spell of cold weather, and knows as well where it is best to be when that happens.
The cat refusing to come into its own house is one that can sense someone in it is going to die.

A white cat is often regarded with fear in some West Country areas. A white kitten, given to a resident of Moretonhampstead, was seen by a local lady who recoiled in horror saying, "Surelye, you aint gwain to keep that thing! You won't ave no more luck if you do. It's most unlucky to keep a white cat; there's most sure to be death in the ouze avore the year's out."

In strict contrast, some people in the same area consider that a black cat will bring luck with it, especially if it comes to the house of its own accord.

It is not only in life that the cat has uses in the home. A dried, mummified cat found in the rafters of a thatched cottage in Axminster was a reminder, like one found at Corfe Mullen, near Wimborne, that cats were sometimes crucified and put into the roof space of a cottage to protect the home from witches. While clearing the cottage roof-space, before treating dry rot in rafters, 'Rentokil' men discovered the Axminster cat, well preserved, and in a very good condition, except that its tail was broken off. The front paws were separated, one to each side of the body, as if the cat might have been nailed through them, but there was no clear evidence of this. It did however still display teeth, and the body was still covered in a leathery skin following more than three hundred years of 'protection duty' for those who have lived on the premises. The building dates from around 1634 and the cat was probably put into the attic as a protector, when the cottage was built.

Mummified cats are not often found as far west as Axminster but in the cottage next door, a similar, dried, cat had been discovered some years earlier when roofing work was undertaken on those premises.

In 1965 a dried cat was found when a cottage was being re-thatched at Woodbury. It was complete and, from its position and pose when found, it was clearly seen that the animal could not have arrived there alive; it had obviously been killed and placed *in situ*.

A dried cat was found during renovations being made to an old farmhouse at Higher Brimley in 1970; it was found walled up, beside the old bake-oven, by the hearth-fire.

BIRDS AND GHOSTLY BEASTS

In rural areas the lore of birds is often referred to: for signs of sorrow or joy; for indications of weather changes; for the arrival or departure of good fortune; or a sign to warn that work should cease and preparations begin to greet an imminent visitor.

Ghostly beasts are reputed to guard some Devon churches and churchyards from the undesirable attentions of witches, or worse. In the parish of Lew Trenchard, according to the Rev Baring-Gould and as already mentioned, the guardians are said to be two white pigs yoked together with a silver chain. In an adjoining parish it is a black dog that is claimed to be in spiritual residence, and in yet another rural parish, a calf is said to act as protector to the church.

As a footnote to these comments we should perhaps add, briefly, that while the particularly imperious cat is considered to have predictive powers, other animals too share such abilities. Dogs and horses, among four-legged friends, birds, bees and many creatures can warn when evil might seek to become your companion; as guides, or providers of warnings, the friends in the animal kingdom so often taken for granted rarely fail us; in this life or the next.

A friend of ours in Hampshire communicates regularly with her animal companions of previous years, animals that have 'passed over', but who still, to our personal knowledge, visit her.

A cat that once chose us to live with, remains close by, often seen, his presence undoubted.

For such beliefs a few short years ago, we, and many like us, would have faced accusations of being witches.

PAINT AND POWDER WITCHCRAFT

All women, of whatever age, rank, profession, or degree, whether virgins, maids or widows, that shall, from and after such Act, impose upon, seduce, and betray into matrimony, any of His Majesty's subjects, by the scents, paints, cosmetic washes, artificial teeth, false hair, Spanish-wool, iron stays, hoops, high heeled shoes, bolstered hips, shall incur the penalty of law in force against witchcraft.

Law of England 1770

MOB RULE

It is seldom that a poor wretch is brought to trial for witchcraft but that there is at the heels of her a popular rage that does little less than demand her to be put to death, and if a judge is so clear and open as to declare against that impious vulgar opinion, that the devil himself has the power to torment and kill innocent children, or that he is pleased to divert himself with the good people's cheese, butter, pigs, and geese, and the like errors of the foolish rabble, the countryman, the jury, cry this judge hath no religion, for he doth not believe in witches, and so, to show that they have some, they hang the poor wretches.

Lord Keeper Guildford

ADVICE FROM THE PAST - FOR YOUR PROTECTION

On meeting a suspected witch the thumb of each hand was turned inward, and the finger closed upon it; care was also taken to let her have the wall-side, or best path.

Caution was used that gloves, or any portion of apparel worn next to the skin, came not into the possession of a witch, as it was strongly believed she had an highly ascendant power over the rightful owner.

A bit of witch-wood, or a hare's foot, was carried in the pocket, under an impression that the possessor was free from any harm that otherwise might accrue from the old hag's malignant practices.

One thing of importance was not to go out of the house in a morning without taking a bite of bread, cake, or other eatable to break the fast.

A thick white curtain was hung inside the window to prevent an 'evil eye' being cast into the room.

Although the practices aforementioned are spoken of in the past tense, they are not, at the present time, altogether done away; July 30th 1827

Extracts from *Recollections of Practices Formerly used To avert and Avoid The Power of Witches. The Table Book of 1827*

THE ORDER OF THE (WITCHES') GARTER

According to the popular tale, the establishment of the Order of The Garter came about after Edward III gallantly retrieved the garter of his dancing partner, the Countess of Salisbury after it fell to the floor, much to her embarrassment. The King picked up the garter and tied it to his own leg, saying "*Honi soit qui mal y pense*", (shame to him who thinks ill). In that incident some suggest that the King found inspiration for the Order of the Garter, while others add that his knowledge of Witchcraft and sympathy for it was revealed.

The garter had long since been regarded as a sign associated with a witch, so is it significant that Edward founded the Order with himself at the head of twelve Knights, and his son also at the head of twelve Knights; two sets of thirteen people. Furthermore, the King's mantle contained 168 garters depicted within its design, to add to the garter he wore; thirteen times thirteen.

Could it be that a King at play was protecting the Old Religion, when a garter fell to the floor, revealing his partner to be a witch ?

BROOMSTICK WITCHCRAFT

Witches are often depicted as flying through the air on a broomstick. Broom, the plant, was originally tied to a stick to be used for sweeping and was also a plant that appeared on the badge of the Plantaganets, rulers - who it is said - favoured the Old Religion. The broom handle, or stick, was easily recognised as a phallic symbol. With the broom attached, the coupling was believed to clearly demonstrate the sexual act, which suggests the true significance of sticks and brooms used by witches past and present.

Similarly, the belief points to a relevance for the brooms and sticks that appear so often in the folk-dance and morris-dance rites that the public find quaintly English and entertaining today. Unrecognised by most, the broom and stick, jumped over, danced around, or held on high, perpetuate fertility rituals performed in ancient times, by pre-Celtic peoples.

To 'marry over the broomstick' brought recognition to an irregular marriage in which the partners jumped over the broom to confirm their common-law act of union. The gypsy wedding, with the couple jumping back and forth across the broom, suggests further recognition of fertility rituals. Across the country, a belief in one region that it is unlucky for an unmarried woman to step across a broomstick is balanced in others where the belief is that only married woman should perform a broomstick dance; either way the fertility connotations come to the fore.

THE MARK OF THE CONDEMNED

Body blemishes are often ignored today. Those that are considered to be actually, or even potentially, psychologically damaging can be dealt with medically, either removed altogether or reduced.

The specialists who deal with them in the twentieth century are likely to be sympathetic to the person to whom the blemish has become a problem. The 'experts' who considered such blemishes in the seventeenth century felt no such compassion. A mole, a flea bite, a wart - even a pimple - would be enough for the professional witch-finder to provide a court with conclusive evidence of the guilt of the poor possessor of such a natural mark.

Witch-finding was an enterprise born out of fear, exploited by its practitioners up and down the country, and conducted with vigour. The rewards for a witch-finder were enormous in times when a good day's pay could be less than 2p of today's money. Fees provided to witch-finders for their services are recorded from as 'little' as £6 for clearing a town of its witches, to £15 for a professional approach to be presented to the problem of witches; an approach that proved satisfactory to many a mayor or town leader.

Stowmarket is recorded as paying a witchfinder £23 for services rendered. The professional approach of the witch-finder was not above including the use of retractable spikes that disappeared into a handle. The instrument provided irrefutable confirmation of the victim's guilt to anyone who watched the proceedings. When the witch-finder applied the spike to a dubious wart and encouraged the official onlooker to observe, most carefully, that the metal spike penetrated the body fully, then re-emerged without so much as a drop of blood being seen, the demonstration guaranteed that the witch-finder would depart the town with a full purse.

A supernumerary nipple found on a male or a female, was a bonus. Here was evidence which proved, undoubtedly, that the possessor could suckle the devil himself. Once a blemish was found on the body of a victim, there was little chance that the witch-finder would not succeed in extracting a confession of witchcraft from them.

The use of the rack was illegal, but other methods of torture were just as effective. Starvation would add to the pain of enduring days and nights without sleep. Solitary confinement could be combined with being tied hand and foot for days on end, while enforced walking, up and down a cell or round and round a room, could continue until the victim collapsed, was revived, and continued again until collapsing again; finally if not fatally, for death's release was denied them as long as possible. Witch-finders considered that confession was inevitable, however unbelievable those confessions may appear to be today, and the records confirm that they were probably right. Across the country witch-finders forced wild admissions from innocent women. In East Anglia Rebecca West confessed to being married to the Devil. Elizabeth Clarke confessed to having slept with the Devil many times over a seven-year period and, even while in gaol, she claimed to have been 'visited by a black imp'.

In August 1682, at Exeter, Susanna Edwards confessed that she had welcomed the devil to her bed and that he had appeared to her as a young boy, "who did lie with me and suck at my breast". She also confessed to meeting the Devil again, in a lane between Bideford and Abbotsham, in which he led her away and "did suck blood from her breast".

There was no escape from such wild confessions and many paid the ultimate penalty after making them. Susanna Edwards was hanged at Heavitree, together with two other condemned 'witches', Temperance Lloyd and Mary Trembles, all three from Bideford.

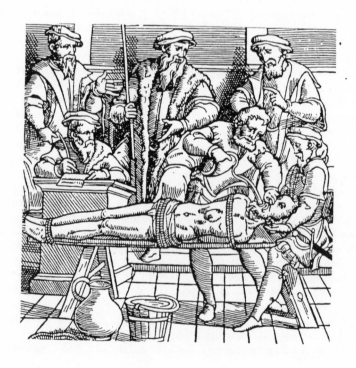

THE HAND OF GLORY

A disembodied, burned skeletal hand was found in the ruins of an old cottage near Slimbridge in Gloucestershire when a motorway was being built. It was decreed to have been a 'hand of glory'. Belief in the powers of these gruesome objects is recorded in Ireland as well as England, and various countries in Europe, and in all areas the use of such objects was attributed to witches and robbers. The basic requirement of a human hand was supplied by resurrectionists, or even murderers, who cut the hands from corpses.

One of two alternatives would then be applied by the user of the 'hand'. A special candle, in a holder, was sometimes fixed into the hand. One such holder is to be found in the Museum of Witchcraft in Boscastle, Devon. It is probably coincidental that, when we last visited the museum, a skeletal hand was displayed close to the candle-holder exhibit, but the bones of that hand had not suffered the burning that a Hand of Glory would have shown.

The Slimbridge hand did show every sign of being used as a candle itself in which case, after particular preparation that need not be detailed here, the outspread fingers and thumb had been set alight to burn slowly. Throughout the western counties there were many demands made for a 'hand of glory', once the cause of a problem had been confirmed.

Scrofula, the skin disease often referred to as the King's Evil, was regularly confused by early doctors with ulcers, or even barber's rash. Witches advised that a method of accurately diagnosing the disease was for the afflicted person to dig up a fresh worm from the garden and place it on the offensive sore; if the worm turned purple and died within minutes, the witch told them, they would know that scrofula was their problem. All that was needed then, was a cure.

Cures for the disease were not easy to come by, but that didn't stop them taking the witch's advice that wherever the dead could be found, so too could a cure.

After the wreck of the S S *Uppingham*, in November 1890, the bodies recovered were temporarily placed, some under the belfry of Hartland Church and some in a stable. The Vicar of Hartland reported to the Shipwrecked Fishermen and Mariners' Society, of which he was local honorary agent, that the hand from one of the bodies was superstitiously used by a villager for striking the King's Evil. The effectiveness of a cure brought about by using a 'dead hand' was referred to by Scot in his *Discoverie of Witchcraft* in which he wrote: "To heal the king's or queen's evil, or any other soreness of the throat, first touch the place with the hand of one that died an untimely death."

If the 'hand' cure was considered less than attractive, an alternative means of trying to secure a cure for the King's Evil was for the sufferer to attend the birth of a child and have the infant's hand passed three times over the afflicted area as soon after birth as possible.

The Reverend R F Meredith, Vicar of Halstock, near Crewkerne, wrote in June 1883 to *The Times* with an account of what he considered to be a case of witchcraft.

> *In a parish where the counties of Devon, Dorset, and Somerset meet, a young man, being affected with scrofula which caused at times contraction of the muscles of the right thigh and very considerable pain, formed the idea that a poor delicate woman living next door, the wife of a labourer and mother of several children, had bewitched him, and one day in his agony rushed into her house with a large sewing needle, and before the woman had time to think, scratched her severely in the neck and in four places on her bare arm, drawing blood in each instance, and ran off. The poor woman came to me to complain, showing the scratches, and I advised her to take out a summons before the justice, but time passed. The young man, as usual, felt relieved of his pain for a time, and his mother, a widow occupying a few acres of land with cows and pigs, tried to assure me that drawing the blood cured her son, for she considered the other woman had overlooked him.*

TO REPEL A WITCH ...

In Devon and Dorset a bitch deprived of all motherly qualities (by the, often inexpert, removal of all internal reproductive organs) was considered to be the only animal that could be used successfully to hunt out or repel a witch. If such a creature was not readily available, other means were, and finding out who was a witch rarely seems to have been a problem. The merest hint of their being involved with witchcraft could easily cause a great many fingers of suspicion to be pointed at women, men, and even children.

BLOOD-LETTING

For a witch to lose her own blood is akin to losing her powers. Throughout the country the practice of 'drawing' the blood from a witch, to make them bleed in order to gain protection, is an act that is frequently recorded.

In 1823 at Wiveliscombe, Somerset, a case was recorded that comes near to murder.

Differing from many other cases of blood-letting that involve witches only, this one involved a 'cunning man', known as Old Baker, the Somerset Wizard.

One of two daughters of a woman named Bryant suffered from fits and believed herself to have been possessed and bewitched. The mother took the girl to Old Baker who immediately confirmed that she had been attacked by a witch whom he identified as Mrs Burges, a neighbour of the Bryant family. He prescribed pills and potions to be used and taken by the girl to overcome the effects of witchcraft. Mrs Bryant duly paid the fees Old Baker charged and was provided with the necessary remedies, including an additional packet of herbs.

Old Baker provided the woman with written instructions that the herbs were to be burned, a little at a time, on coals with a little hay and rosemary, and further instructed the woman that, while they were burning, she should first read out loud the opening two verses of the 68th Psalm, and then recite the Lord's Prayer. His advice concluded with the order that the blood of the attacking witch must be drawn, if the girl was to recover completely from her influence.

Mrs Bryant was not a woman to keep things to herself, and soon confided to a neighbour that Mrs Burges was a witch, and one whose blood she had every intention of drawing.

Not surprisingly, Mrs Burges soon heard of the accusation, and the threat, and went to the Bryant home to face her accuser and deny everything. Fortunately, she did not go alone but went there accompanied by a woman friend. As soon as Mrs Burges arrived at the house she was attacked by Mrs Bryant, thrown to the floor and held down by the second daughter while her sister, the bewitched one, tried to stab her with a big nail. As Mrs Burges tried to escape her arms were badly lacerated by the nail. The neighbour accompanying her screamed out for help while trying to drag the nail-wielding girl away from her friend but the mob that swiftly assembled was content to allow the 'blood drawing' to continue.

Word had already spread far and wide that Mrs Burges was a witch, and witches had to be dealt with. By the time Mrs Burges was pulled away, by her one and only friend, from beneath the rain of blows, the nails had slashed almost two dozen blood-riven wounds down her arms, and from wounds in her shoulders and breast blood freely flowed. The blood drawing was complete.

She was attended by a surgeon who dressed her dreadful injuries, and reported the affray. As a result of his intervention Mrs Bryant and her daughters found themselves taken before a judge at Taunton Assizes where the whole story was heard. The judge, in his closing remarks, only regretted that Old Baker had not appeared before him also.

He warned the Wizard that, if he did not leave off his conjuring, and was caught and brought to his court, he would have great pleasure in charming him in a way that the Wizard would undoubtedly not like. The three Bryant women were found guilty, and sentenced to four months' imprisonment.

Near Land's End, in the community of Morvah, lived two elderly women in the almshouses there. It was nearing the end of the nineteenth century, and they had known each other for many years. There was no love lost between them, each blaming the other for the individual and personal misfortunes they had suffered during a hard lifetime. One of the women considered the other to be a witch. When she fell ill one winter, for no obvious reason, she believed that the 'witch', who lived next door, was the cause of her misfortune and was convinced that her enemy of old had cast a spell on her. Determined to escape the 'witch's' clutches and drive her out of the community once and for all, she waited for the woman to pass her door, on her way to visit others in the village.

The sick woman, clutching a rusty nail in her hand, sat at her window as the hours passed, watching for the witch to return. When at last the old woman did come back to the almshouses and approached her own door she was attacked by a demented figure who shouted and screamed in triumph as she plunged the rusty nail into her arm. The witch's blood was spilled, as had been the intention.

The incident caused an uproar. Local people took sides. The vicar threatened the old woman that he would swear out a summons if she tried to harm her neighbour again. The doctor proclaimed that the supposed 'witch' could not have caused the illness suffered by the old woman. However, the woman recovered, miraculously many said, immediately after spilling the 'witch's' blood.

In the first part of *Henry VI*, Shakespeare illustrates the way of disposing of a witch, in Act One, Scene Five:

> *[Here an alarum again, and Talbot pursueth the Dauphin and driveth him.*
> *Then enter, Joan La Pucelle, driving Englishmen before her. Then enter Talbot]*
> Tal.*Where is my strength, my valour,*
> *and my force ?*
> *Our English troops retire, I cannot stay them;*
> *A woman clad in armour, chaseth them.*
> *[Enter La Pucelle]*
> *Here she comes. I'll have a bout with thee;*
> *Devil or devil's dam, I'll conjure thee;*
> *Blood will I draw on thee - thou art a witch -*
> *And straightway give thy soul to him thou serv'st.*

In 1924, over three hundred years after this was written, a Devonshire farmer was prosecuted for just such an assault on a woman neighbour whom he had accused of being a witch.

The court heard the farmer claim in his defence that the woman had ill-wished him and had bewitched his pig and because of this his attack on her was totally justified. The woman gave evidence that, for some reason entirely unknown to her, the farmer had appeared behind her one day, had taken hold of her and stabbed her arm repeatedly with a pin. When she broke away from his grasp he had taken up a gun and threatened to shoot her. All of this time, she added, he had shouted loudly that he was drawing the blood of a witch, which distressed her immensely.

When taken into custody the farmer had demanded that the police should raid the home of the woman where they would find a crystal ball and other magical paraphernalia to provide conclusive evidence that the woman was a witch, and that he was entirely justified in acting as he had to protect himself, and his pig. Nothing in the records suggest that the raid took place. The farmer's story was not believed and he was sentenced to one month in gaol.

In the December 1884 edition of Crossing's *Western Antiquary*, a case is reported as put before the Sherborne magistrates in which a married woman named Tamar Humphries, of Cold Harbour, was accused of attacking an old lady on 19 September of that year, with the intention of drawing her blood. The woman Tamar violently attacked was Sarah Smith, an 83-year-old who was dependent upon Parish Relief, and who lived next door to her.

The magistrates heard that Tamar's daughter was a confirmed invalid who suffered severely from rheumatism, and that Tamar believed her daughter had been bewitched by Sarah Smith.

It seems, from the report, that Sarah was well known in the area and was considered by her other neighbours to be a quiet, inoffensive member of their community. She had been in her garden, digging potatoes, when she had been set upon by the defendant who caught her roughly by the shoulders, saying, "Oh! you Sal Smith, what's thee done to my daughter? I'll draw blood of thee." Tamar Humphries then repeatedly stabbed old Sarah's arms and hands with a needle, making them bleed, while shouting at the old woman that she was a witch and that she was drawing her blood, for 'witching' her daughter.

In another case, reported in the *Dorset County Chronicle*, July 1887, a working man had been convinced that all of his health problems and the mishaps that had plagued him were caused by his having been bewitched by his next-door neighbour, another inoffensive old lady who indignantly refuted his accusations. The man was not to be pacified and with a sharpened reap-hook in his hand was about to attack the old woman, to draw her blood and break her spell, when interference by a third party prevented him from carrying out his plan.

Similar cases no doubt were known to Thomas Hardy who included a vivid description of the cruel practice of 'blooding' in his Wessex novel, *Return of the Native*, in which Susan Nonsuch violently attacks Eustacia Vye with the intention drawing blood. Susan stabs and pricks the wayward and ill-fated young woman repeatedly while under the delusion that the girl has bewitched her children; and Hardy set the scene for this witchcraft attack in a church.

William Barnes, in his delightful descriptions of rustic Dorset life, did not omit to include the Craft when he wrote of rural ways of life, customs, ideas and beliefs. In the following extract drawn from his poetic tale about witchcraft, he manages in a humorous way to convey that the problems they caused could increase with the effort of getting rid of 'A Witch'.

An' zoo, they soon began to vind
That she's agone an' left behind
Her evil wish that had such pow'r,
That she did meake their milk an' eäle turn zour,
An' addle all the eggs their vowls did lay;
They coulden vetch the butte in the churn,

An' all the cheese begun to turn
All back ageän to curds an' whey;
The little pigs, a runnèn' with the zow,
Did zicken, somehow, nobody know'd how,
An' avll, an' turn their snouts toward the sky,
An' only gie woone little grunt an' die.
An' all the little ducks an' chicken
Wer death-struck out in the yard a-pickèn
Their bits o' food, an vell upon their head,
An' flapp'd their little wings an' drapp'd down dead.
They coulden fat the calves, they woulden thrive;
They coulden seave their lambs alive;
Their sheep were all a-coath'd[1], or gied noo wool;
The horses vell away to skin an' bwones,
An' got so weak they coulden pull
A half a peck o' stwones.
The dog got dead-alive and drowsy,
The cat vell zick an' woulden mousy;
An' every time the vo'k went up to bed,
They wer a-hag-rod till they wer half dead.
They us'd to keep her out o' the house, tis true,
A-naïlen up at door a hosses shoe;
An' I've a-heärd the farmer's wife did try
To dawk[2] a needle or a pin
In the drough her wold, hard, wither'd skin,
An draw her blood, a-comèn by;
But she could never vetch a drap,
For pins would ply[3] an' needless snap
Ageän her skin; an that in coo'se
Did meäke the hag bewitch em woo'se.

[1] suffering from a liver disease
[2] prick
[3] bend

9 Witchcraft among Plants and Trees

For those fortunate enough actually to live in the countryside, where Celtic influences can be clearly seen and where hidden knowledge is still retained, ancient wisdom guides those who choose to see, with open eyes, the natural way of things. However, knowledge that can be found on one's own doorstep may not easily be seen, or sought.

Those tribes that first tramped the wild and windswept West Country, worshipped Nature, understood her ways, lived by her guidance and benefited fom her bounty. The knowledge given to these people by their Gods was vital to life; but new Gods came, brought by those who decreed that the old ways were a heresy.

For those who lived in later centuries, when the forests had gone, the wisdom of their predecessors remained as they strayed down varying paths away from the ways of Nature, the seasons, the moon and stars, the sun, and time itself.

For those who kept alive the understanding of the medicines that wild plants provide, of the values of the trees and of bushes, and of berries, nuts and fruits that could be relied upon, a knowledge already forgotten by most, their fate was to be hounded as witches, and their reward was an agonising death.

But the knowledge possessed by the wise ones survived. Within these pages we can only offer others a starting point perhaps, for a worthwhile journey through the wise craft contained in Nature's store.

Latter-day health foods and natural medicines have their origins in knowledge used by our Celtic ancestors thousands of years ago, and used continuously ever since. In the fifth century BC the Greek doctor Hippocrates listed 400 herbs in use; Dioscorides wrote a herbal in the first century AD that extended the list to 600 herbs; and the knowledge recorded by herbalist Thomas Culpeper in the seventeenth century is now being taken forward by new 'discoverers of Nature's wisdom', into the twenty-first century.

As the crafts of the wise ones are learned, used and enjoyed, a respect for Nature and her ways comes with that learning, for good reason.

NIGHTSHADE

Nightshade has been used by unscrupulous power-seekers throughout history to induce madness and death in any who oppose them. Nightshade, it is said, can helps people gain 'second sight', inducing clairvoyance, and can empower people to fly. The first application is politics; the second witchcraft.

Throughout the country, nightshade is a plant of mystery, with an evil, deadly reputation; yet a collar of nightshade was said to save cattle from enchantment and, twisted in a wreath with holly, it was said to be a certain cure for hag-ridden horses.

The distilled juice of the whole herb was used to relieve the swelling of testicles; human probably, rather than equine. The juice was also said to be good for treating ringworm and shingles and, if dropped into the ears, it eased pains that arose from inflammation; it was also good for swelling under the throat.

Humans could wear a wreath of the plant around their brow to defeat spells placed upon them by witches, or to help evade the influence of those who possessed the ability to 'overlook' them or to avoid the Evil Eye being cast upon them.

Since nightshade has a well-earned lethal reputation, it is right to remind readers that it remains a wisdom in the countryside to ensure that everyone, from an early age, is able to recognise both varieties of the plant and that while the 'common' nightshade provides valued medicinal benefits, it needs to be handled with care, used moderately, and not confused with its 'deadly' cousin. Be aware that common nightshade is bad enough, but that deadly nightshade is the plant with a lethal nature, and that each of the nightshades needs to be readily recognised, clearly known, identified beyond doubt, and not touched. This is not a witch's warning, just countryside commonsense.

Culpeper, the most renowned collector of herbal lore and collator of knowledge, warned of the perils that just the touch of deadly nightshade can inflict.

A lady, troubled by a small, possibly cancerous, ulcer below one of her eyes, applied a portion of green leaf to it one night and, by morning, the uvea of that eye was so affected that the pupil would not contract in the brightest light.

Fortunately, her other eye remained unaffected and when the piece of deadly nightshade leaf was removed from the ulcer the afflicted eye was gradually restored to its original state.

The moral of this tale is: *beware of all nightshades and do not touch*. A little knowledge can be a dangerous thing.

ELDER

A possible link between Old and New Religions, rather than witchcraft, may be discerned in the fact that older Devonians consider that the cross on which Jesus suffered and died had been made of elder.

Their Warwickshire and Somerset counterparts add that they believe that Judas hanged himself on an elder tree. These particular beliefs may also explain why so many people across the entire country feel that when elder is brought into the home, it brings bad luck with it.

The general reluctance to use it for fire-wood in the west meant that there was little or no reason to give it house room. In Dorset, the burning of elder wood was considered to be the witch's way of raising the Devil but having the tree planted near a grave would protect the dead person. Similarly, the magical properties of elder would protect a household from witches; but even then the wood was secured to the outside of the house where it would be clearly visible to any approaching witches.

Some of the early settlers in America had family origins in the West Country and it was out there, before and after the states united, that elder wood was used to identify witches in ways that were reminiscent of those often used in this country.

A small piece of elder would first be dipped in oil, and then set alight, while being allowed to float on water in an earthen basin; the elements of earth, fire and water would combine their forces to turn the wood to point at any witch nearby.

BLACKBERRIES

Some of Nature's growing gifts to the wise ones could be used completely. The blackberry, known to wise women for hundred of years, is but one example with its leaves, buds, flowers, fruit, and even its brambles all providing foods, remedies and curative values of all kinds.

Culpeper considers, among many possible applications that, "powder of the root is good to break or drive forth gravel and the stone in the reins and kidneys . . . the leaves and brambles, as well green as dry, are excellent good lotions for sores in the mouth or secret parts . . . the distilled water of the fruit is very pleasant to taste and very effectual in fevers and hot distempers" of the body, head, eyes and other parts.

Humans and sick animals, were often passed beneath a bramble arch, formed by lifting up a branch rooted at both ends, to cure illnesses:

Under the bramble, let thorns be rough,
On them I leave the whooping cough.

All parts of the plant were collected and dried for use throughout the year and it was the timing of the collecting of the fruit which gave rise to certain custom and belief.

The Devil might not have power enough to interfere with the curative values contained in the blackberries, but he could limit the time they were available, and useful. In some areas the Devil is said to spit on blackberries; West Country variations suggest that the Devil does this sometimes as early as Michaelmas, 29 September, so do conflicting 'relatively local' dates cancel out the custom? Not at all. 'Old' Michaelmas Day is 10 October. Ancient custom preceded the Christian calendar by a long way, and a belief of some kind, co-existing with the Old Religion, had the 'Devil' connections grafted on to it later by advocates of Christianity.

In August 1925 *The Bideford Gazette* gave space to the comment that, "there is an ancient belief that blackberries must be gathered before September 20th, for on that date every year the Devil leaves his mark on the berries which are still growing, and people who are foolish enough to pick the fruit after that date are certain to fall into the hands of his Satanic Majesty, and to suffer misfortune, ere the year is out."

THE ROWAN TREE

In the western counties, the rowan tree is reputed to hold properties that still provide protection against witches and evil-doing today, just as it always has. Regionally, in much of mid and southern England, the rowan shares that reputation with the hawthorn, whereas in the north of England, much of Wales, Scotland, and the Isle of Man, the rowan remains the mighty tree of protection. "Rowan tree and red threid, Gar the witches tyne their speed."

In Scotland the wood was used in house and farm buildings to permanently 'build-in' its beneficial influence; in England and Wales a branch hung over the door provides good luck to the household while protecting its occupants from witches.

In times when wood was used to fashion most tools used in a Somerset farm dairy a rowan twig in the churn, or a churn staff of rowan, kept the butter safe from evil interference.

A piece of rowan in a Gloucester man's pocket kept him safe from the evil eye, or being 'overlooked'. Cornish carters used rowan whips so that their horses would not be bewitched.

In the West Country the recognition of and respect for the rowan, its values and its many magical properties, particularly those relating to protection, appear to have increased in recent years; or is really just co-incidence that the tree has become popular and that fashion rather than faith is the only reason it now appears in so many gardens and near new homes today ?

Or is it, perhaps, that there are more witches in the West Country than elsewhere?

THE PROVEN TREE

A young ash tree growing in Warwickshire and depicted in an engraving contained in *The Gentleman's Magazine*, October 1804, was believed to have cured the infant son of one Henry Rowe. An article accompanying the picture relates that, in 1791, the infant, Thomas Rowe, was taken to the tree and drawn through the body of it as a means of curing a rupture the child suffered.

The article confirms that tree was split open to enable the child to pass through it, and that the cure succeeded. Thomas, thirteen years of age at that time, was a fit and healthy youth who could clearly be seen to be a living testament to a cure that had long been recommended by wise women, or witches.

10 Fairies at the Bottom of the Garden?

As often as not, the accusations made against anyone, male or female, that they were practitioners of witchcraft, were made by an enemy of the accused. Whether the enmity was founded on fear or oppression, jealousy or bigotry, through the centuries one person slighted by another, or harmed in some way would often take their revenge by making a public accusation that directed attention towards the person who was the object of their hatred.

Alternatively, the person accused was often brought to trial on witchcraft charges for expressing their own unnatural or supernatural claims. One such case is recorded in the Bodleian Library, Oxford, regarding the imprisonment of a young woman in Bodmin gaol; an imprisonment brought about by her own, unusual, confessions.

Anne Jeffries, a poor man's child, was born in St Teath, near Helstone, appropriately enough, since many similarly-named places seem to be associated with the unusual. Following the custom of the time in the county of Cornwall, Anne was taken into the home of a more prosperous local family. This tradition helped the workless families in the community, providing children with food, clothes, a bed and the occasional coin, in return for their services in the household, until the 'apprentice' came of age; then at 21 years.

Anne was a bright child, adventurous and boisterous, who enjoyed her childhood and youthful years in the Cornish home of Moses Pitt, a London publisher. When she was nineteen years old, in 1645, she had been sitting one afternoon in arbour in the garden, knitting, when she was suddenly taken ill, and seized with what appeared to be a fit.

She was found in a convulsive condition beside a flowerbed by members of the Pitt family who hastily carried her to the house, and to the comfort of her bed.

As she recovered she pointed to the window, asking others present if they too had just seen six, small, green-clothed people departing that way. She had met them in the garden, she claimed. The remarks were attributed to a rambling mind, and ignored; but recalled time and again.

Whenever Anne raised the subject of the small, spiritual beings who visited her, describing them clearly, she was encouraged to go to church to pay her devotions.

Anne persisted with her story, saying that one of the tiny men she had befriended had touched her eyes and taught her how to fly. She described her experiences of flight, and of travelling great distances to visit a strange and beautiful country where she learned many things.

Then Anne discovered that she possessed the power to heal. She was working in the fields when she heard news of a woman who had broken her leg. At once Anne rushed to the injured person. When she arrived a servant was still preparing a horse before riding some eight miles to Bodmin

An incubus embraces a witch in this German woodcut made in 1490. The demon has the face of a handsome young man; only his clawed feet reveal him as a devil in human form

to summon aid from the surgeon, Mr Lobb. Anne found the woman in pain, and offered her help.

The woman was not inclined to allow Anne to treat her injuries but, fearing that her refusal could cause a return of Anne's fits, she finally agreed to allow the girl to do what she could.

Gently stroking the injured leg, Anne advised the woman that she would have no need of the surgeon, that the servant need not ride to Bodmin, and that her touch alone would bring healing.

The woman listened as Anne told her that she had been summoned to help her by six small green-clothed men who visited her in the fields, creatures who were her friends and who visited her often.

It was a story the woman could not believe, until she realised with amazement that her broken bone was healing, just at the touch of the girl. The news of Anne's healing powers spread across Cornwall and people came to her from far and wide to be cured of all manner of ills. Some came all the way from London to see her. Anne denied no one, took no money, and gave credit for the miracles she performed to the small green-clothed people. She would eat no food, for *they* fed her, she said. She would take no drink either, for the same reason.

Magistrates and church ministers examined her, seeking to determine if she was consorting with witches to gain her powers, or was in league with the Devil.

She told them all of her small green-clothed friends and Cornwall's worthies decided that these creatures were evil spirits. Anne desired all who doubted her to turn to their Bible and read in the 1st Epistle of St John, Chapter 4, Verse 1: "Dearly beloved, believe not every spirit, but try the spirits whether they be of God."

She was committed to Bodmin gaol by the infamous magistrate, Jan Tregeagle, steward to the Earl of Radnor.

She had been forewarned by her small green-clothed friends that this would happen and even in gaol Anne would not deny her association with them.

She was kept imprisoned, without food, and later claimed that during her incarceration she was sustained emotionally by her friends who brought her meals to maintain her physical strength during the ordeal.

Justice Tregeagle, who was her greatest persecutor, kept her imprisoned for a considerable time, first in Bodmin gaol and then in his own house, but eventually she was conditionally freed.

Under the terms of her release, Anne went to live near Padstow in the home of a widow, Mrs Frances Tom. There she remained for many years, continuing to perform her healing.

By 1696, Anne Warren, now seventy, and having enjoyed many years of marriage, was living peacefully, but was still considered by some to be a saint, and by others to be a witch.

11 Witch Ways

THE COVEN

Chaucer uses the word 'covent' in his *Canterbury Tales* when referring to a meeting of thirteen people and a reminder of this Latinised version of the word, convent, remains with us in London's Covent Garden.

Depositions presented to Somerset magistrates regarding witchcraft activities taking place in Somerset and Dorset between 1650 and 1654 include some that refer to the witches who held their meetings on Leigh common, in Dorset. This proof of the sisterhood meeting at Leigh, but not the number, adds credibility to the traditional name that is locally still applied at times to the Common: 'Witches' Corner'.

A coven of witches at Wincanton was brought to trial in 1664 and its women members accused of consorting with the Devil who, it was said, appeared to them in various forms and aided them in bringing down harm upon others. Elizabeth Style, one of the witches, admitted to making wax figures of people she intended to harm, and confessed to seeing the Devil appear before her as a man, cat, dog and fly, and in many other guises.

The first use of the word 'coven' to describe such a meeting is attributed to Isobel Goudrie, a witch from Auldearn, near Nairn in Scotland, who, when questioned in 1662 about her disturbing activities and strange colleagues, confessed that, "there are thirteen persons in each coven", and quite quickly it seems the word coven became associated specifically with groups of women who were regarded as being witches.

More covens are mentioned by the Chaplain to King Charles II, Joseph Glanvil, in his work *Sadducismus Triumphatus*, published in 1681. Glanvil's work includes a number of stories that were intended by him to prove the reality of witchcraft in his day, and refers to the Somerset witches who were tried in 1664.

Two covens are mentioned, one at Brewham and another at Wincanton, each containing thirteen members and each governed by a mysterious 'Man in Black' whose identity is not revealed.

The traditional number to form a witches' coven is thirteen, ideally six men, six women and a leader. Covens can, did, and do work well with less than this number, and many witches say that the total number practising the Craft, in a group, should not exceed thirteen.

The lesser known style of coven, with eight member witches, remains popular with Craft practitioners.

When more than thirteen like-minded witches operate in one area, then two covens can be established, to grow to full thirteen in size again, before dividing once again.

By such means the Craft continues to grow and thrive across the south west today.

There is no 'requirement' within the Craft for witches to conform to the coven system, and many experienced, older witches continue to practise the Craft alone. Their experience, however, was probably gained in part from being associated with a coven in earlier years

There are many ways in which the Craft is perpetuated throughout the south west, the country and the world. Equally there are many groups, or covens.

Witchcraft is flourishing, often in response to the recognition of some kind of suppression of, or threat made to Nature by the modern world that is observed by those who care.

We do know of a group of railway witches, and we are also aware that hedgerow witches exist.

There are those covens whose members consider witchcraft to be the Old Religion, and other covens that respond to the coming of the 'new' Aquarian age and dawn of the next millennium.

There are covens that promote a system of aristocracy, with priests, priestesses, witch queens and common witches, and others that do not.

Commercialisation has not crept into the Craft, it has leapt into witchcraft in a big way. Shops proliferate that provide every necessity for following the Craft.

Whatever it is that is needed, charms, oils, candles, incense, books of spells, previously recorded rituals, their mystic sales staff can provide everything; except true knowledge and understanding.

For explorers, a word of advice. Practitioners of the Craft insist that their work can only be used for good, not evil, to help others, not to exploit them.

There is more magic to found in a grove of trees than in a hundred shops.

THE SWIMMING OF WITCHES

Discussing witch-finding, one of the most usual 'memories' we found that we shared with others was a picture that came into all of our minds of white-collared, dark-clothed Puritans pushing an alleged witch into a pond or throwing her into a river to see if she would sink or swim. If she sank and drowned she was obviously innocent, if she survived she could be executed in the sure and certain knowledge that she was a witch. Such incidents, we all agreed, were normal for the seventeenth century, when witch-finders like Matthew Hopkins were about.

The opinion held at that time was that witches, having rejected the water of Christian baptism and salvation, would be rejected by water and would, unnaturally, float.

The test had received royal approval in 1597 when it was recommended by King James I in his book, *Daemonologie*, as a test of witchcraft guilt.

Refinements were added and, instead of people simply throwing the victim into the water, the accused was bound in a special way, their arms

crossed, their thumbs tied to their big toes, and a rope tied round their waist. The latter was to enable them to be pulled out of the water if they sank, but reason suggests that whether they sank or not would depend on who held the rope.

All of this detail still made the swimming of witches a seventeenth-century money-making procedure pursued by witch-finders of the day, or so we thought.

A report contained in William Hone's *Everyday Book*, 1841, confirms that swimming the witch continued long afterwards and describes such an occurrence taking place in 1751.

On 18 April, William Dell, a town crier, proclaimed in the market place that a man and a woman would be publicly ducked for their crimes on the following Monday.

The report confirms that this took place, encouraged by a mob, and that the female 'swimmer' did not survive. An eye witness to her death, a Mr John Holmes, later confirmed that on that day:

> *The man and the woman were separately tied up in cloth or sheet; that a rope was tried under the arm-pits of the deceased, and two men dragged her into the pond; that the men were on one side of the pond, and the other on the other; and they dragged her sheer through the pond several times; and that Colley (one of the men), having a stick in his hand, went into the pond, and turned the deceased up and down several times.*

Another witness, John Humphries, confirmed that:

> *Colley turned her over and over several times with the stick; that after the mob had ducked her several times they brought her to the shore, and set her by the pond side, and then dragged the old man in and ducked him; that after they had brought him to shore, and set him by the pond side, they dragged the deceased in a second time; and that Colley went again into the pond, and turned and pushed the deceased about with his stick as before; that then she being brought to shore again, the man was also a second time dragged in, and underwent the same discipline as he had before; and being brought to shore, the deceased was a third time dragged into the pond; that Colley went into the pond again, and took hold of the cloth or sheet in which she was wrapt, and pulled her up and down the pond till the same came from off her, and then she appeared naked; that then Colley pushed her on the breast with his stick, which she endeavoured with her left hand to catch hold of, but he pulled it away, and that was the last time life was in her.*
>
> *He also deposed that after Colley came out of the pond, he went round among the people who were the spectators of this tragedy, and collected money of them as a reward for the great pains he had taken in showing them sport in ducking the old witch, as he then called the deceased.*

On the 24 August 1751, Thomas Colley was hanged for his crimes but "many thousands stood at a distance to see him die, muttering that it was a hard case to hang a man for destroying an old wicked woman that had done so much mischief by her witchcraft".

We could not attempt to better the words used by William Hone in 1841 when he ended this report. "Ignorance is mental blindness."

HUMAN SACRIFICE

Stories and tales of the past that have earned the reputation for holding that 'grain of truth' that is passed down through the ages to become 'folklore' confirm that the lamb, among other animals, was used in sacrificial celebration. At spring festivals, summer solstice, and in most pre-Christian, natural, rites and rituals, the tales leave little doubt that animals of all kind played their part. Our sole first-hand account of Druidism in action is contained in the writings of Pliny who, after describing a mistletoe-gathering ceremony adds the information that two white bulls were brought forward and sacrificed. Animal sacrifice, not human.

The finding of Druidic metal face masks at Bath, similar to those found in other countries where it was known that they were worn by 'sacrificers', appears to 'confirm' that human sacrifice was 'probably' performed by the Druids.

Excavations at Wilsford and Swanwick revealed shafts in which artefacts were carbon-dated to 1400BC and both the pre-Celtic shafts and later ones contained human remains, probably from sacrifice. Caesar's accounts of mass sacrifice practised by the Celtic Druids is perhaps somewhat jaundiced,

A witch promises to sacrifice children to the Devil

and definitely not a record of sacrifices observed, but a present-day expert on Celtic traditions, Caitlin Matthews, pulls no punches in expressing her opinion that there appear to have been four forms of sacrificial death practised by the Celts: hanging, drowning, cremation and live burial.

Carried over from the pre-Celtic times, quite certainly, was the custom of burying alive a child or youth in the foundations of a new building. Stonehenge and Avebury bear witness to such sacrifice; and so does a church in Devon.

Undisputable evidence of a human sacrifice was found during the course of extensive restoration work being carried out in 1884/85 on Holsworthy Church.

Workmen, taking down the south-west angle wall of the church found a skeleton embedded in the mortar and stone. The wall of this portion of the church was known to be faulty and had settled but, according to the account given by the masons whose work revealed the ghastly remains, and of the architect who supervised the work, there was no trace found of a tomb.

The Rev Baring-Gould believed that the human remains that were found however showed evidence that the person had been buried alive, and speedily. "A mass of mortar was over the mouth, and the stones were huddled about the corpse as though hastily heaped about it."

The author of *Notes on Devon Churches*, Miss B F Cresswell, suggested that the human remains may be a grim relic of the original building of the Norman chapel, and a reminder of beliefs held in those times that it was necessary for such buildings to be erected, quite literally, on the foundation of life.

With that life sealed within, the building of the Norman wall appears to have then been leisurely proceeded with, and the erection of the building completed.

SUCCESSION TO THE CRAFT

Always be wary of wise women, but never be more wary than when they claim to be the seventh daughter of the seventh daughter of a seventh daughter.

In 1876 an article in the *Western Morning News* of 17 June, was drawn to the attention Devonshire Association members:

At the meeting of Plympton Board of Guardians yesterday, Mr C. Bewes said that in consequence of a request from the relieving officer, Mr. Pearse, he had visited a pauper woman named Whiddon, living at Plympton. She had mentioned that she had paid a Mrs. Cox, a herbalist, of Plymouth, a sovereign to cure her. She had received some medicine, and was to get some more from the herbalist, which she was to bury underground, and that would make her quite well. In company with Mr. Pearse, Mr. Bewes said he went to the house of Mrs. Cox, in Cambridge Lane, and told her he was a magistrate, and asked her if Mrs. Whiddon had not consulted her. The herbalist said she (Mrs. Cox) was a clever person, and knew more than most people; and in order to show conclusively that this was the case, and get rid of any scepticism there might have been on the part of Mr. Bewes and Mr. Pearse, she stated, as an explanatory fact, that she was the seventh daughter of the seventh daughter of the seventh daughter. She also observed that she was in the habit of curing scores of people that medical men had given up, and many that Dr. Square and Dr. Hingston had declared to be incurable. People came from all parts of the county to have their cows cured. After that she gave a history of herself and her occupation and Mr. Bewes informed her that he had come there on Mrs. Whiddon's behalf, and demanded the sovereign. The seventh daughter of the other daughters immediately handed it over, and the relieving officer was now in possession of it.

12 Death and the Undead

The customs, traditions, and beliefs that surround death, the only other experience that all humans are guaranteed to share after birth, are wide ranging and usually comforting, at a time when comfort is needed - at least by those who, as yet, remain on the mortal side of the great divide.

Less local 'public notice' is given today of the occurrence of a death than in previous years when the death-knell tolled but even in those times, according to custom in some areas of Devon, a 'passing' bell should not be tolled after sunset.

When a person died a bottle was placed on the windowsill of the room where the corpse lay, 'to catch the angel's tears', and remained there for forty days and nights before being removed; the corpse of course having long since departed.

The grave-diggers knew with the tolling of the bells that their services were required but their work was watched by others for other omens; if a grave was left open over a Sunday, three more would be needed before the week was out.

The fear of an open grave is not unusual, and one left open over the weekend is said to be a precursor of, at least, bad luck. An incident that took place in Devon in 1932 was recorded by Christina Hole in 1955. A funeral had been arranged for the Monday and, contrary to advice, the sexton dug the grave ready on Saturday and refused to even cover it over for the weekend. On the Monday, as family and mourners stood waiting for the funeral procession to come into church, the churchwarden dropped dead in the aisle.

Preparations for the burial of the deceased invokes many of the customs and traditions. The custom already mentioned of ensuring that a 'complete' body is buried extended sometimes to precautions being taken much earlier in life to ensure that this could be achieved.

Amputated limbs are known to have been preserved in Whitstone where it was recorded that a farmworker's finger, cut off in a chaff machine, and several toes that belonged to various carpenters, had been carefully kept for an eventual reunion, and burial, with their owners.

Among Devon funeral customs was one which called for two coins to be placed at the feet of the departed, one on each foot. Some regarded this as a means of ensuring prosperity for the deceased in the next world while others considered that the coins were a distraction for witches who would remove them and leave the dead in peace. The accepted coinage at the turn of the century was farthings for infants who died under three months of age. As an extra precaution, for the protection of their innocent souls, a hole was bored through the coin to confuse the Devil. Two halfpenny coins were placed at the feet of children between three and six months and pennies used for those aged between six months and a year.

From the age of one year and onwards the coins used to assist the departed were required to contain silver and the silver threepenny piece was most commonly used.

With the deceased prepared, as far as humanly possible, the unseen work of helping the dead continues according to the custom when the souls of relatives of the dead person are despatched from the 'other world' to fetch their kinfolk and lead them to their grave with the help of 'corpse candles'. These appear to be similar to ordinary candles, albeit there are small ones for deceased children and large ones for adults, but corpse candles burn with a blue flame and never burn away.

All under the stars, and beneath the green tree,
All over the sward, and along the cold lea,
A little blue flame, a-fluttering came;
It came from the churchyard for you or for me.

I sit by the cradle, my baby's asleep,
And rocking the cradle, I wonder and weep,
O little blue light in the dead of the night,
O prithee, O prithee, no nearer to creep.

Why follow the church path, why steal you this way?
Why halt in your journey, on the threshold why stay?
With flicker and flare, why dance up the stair?
Oh I would! Oh I would! It were dawning of day.

All under the stars and along the green lane,
Unslaked by the dew, and unquenched by the rain,
Of little flames blue to the churchyard steal two,
The soul of my baby! now from him is ta'en.

The actual day decided upon for a funeral could affect a family since it was considered unlucky for the household if a corpse remained on the premises over a Sunday, but if this could not be avoided every precaution was taken to ensure the body was removed before the following Friday. In August 1972, a burial at Broadhembury was postponed from the original day planned when the vicar was informed that the deceased lady could not be buried on that day, because it was her birthday.

Despite the corpse-candle-carrying relatives beckoning, the route taken to its final resting place could still be influenced by the corpse. A somewhat curious perambulation with the corpse used, apparently, to take place on the road from Churston Ferrers Church to the ancient churchyard of Brixham The 'lich-road' was on the funereal route taken by many parishioners. Their friends, bearing them to their last resting place, would ensure that the corpse was carried, with due reverence, around a pile of stones near the start of the lich-road, not far from the church. The stones replaced a cross which had once marked the proposed site of a church. Legend suggests that the devil intervened and the church was not built, but for centuries a corpse was never laid to rest without first passing by where the church might have been.

Such traditions have not grown without encountering objections.

A little over a century ago it was still an old funeral custom at Manaton to carry the corpse three times around a cross near the church-door before burial. The rector disliked the unusual practice and tried in vain to exert his powers and dissuade local families from following the tradition. Finally, determined to take matters into his own hands, he decided to destroy the cross. Overnight it simply disappeared - only the stump of the old granite cross remaining at the church door - and no one ever discovered the whereabouts of the rest.

At some Devon funerals, a count was kept of the numbers of mourners attending the service, to ensure that an even number went through the lichgate. It was thought that the odd one out, when an odd number passed through, was the Devil's disciple looking for someone to meet his master before the year was out. If it meant keeping the numbers even, it was not uncommon for a child to be refused admission to the funeral service.

RITES OF PASSAGE

The practice of expressing consideration for the deceased by giving flowers is simply a relatively modern version of providing food and drink for the departed for their use in the next world. Such pagan rites sit comfortably in our imagination when we think of pre-Christian societies despatching their loved ones to some pagan haven for the dead, burying them with bow and arrow, bowls, tools and an assortment of necessities required in the after-life. An Egyptian tomb, opened to reveal the remains of food among the luxurious trappings that accompanied the dead on their longest journey, would cause hardly a moment's thought nowadays - after all, it was their custom to provide these things.

In Devon something of the sort is still done to this day. A highly respected funeral director confided to me that while it is quite normal to ensure that items such as false teeth are included in a coffin for burial, the inclusion of other things is far from unusual.

In 1994, a well-known country character in mid-Devon died at a fairly good age. Billy, as I shall respectfully call him, was extremely well known for his abilities to heal. By using charms, the laying on of hands, or by uttering an oath, his abilities to conjure up cures were many and varied, established many decades ago, and used throughout his long life to help both people and animals.

[One of the authors can personally testify to his efficacy in providing comfort from pain, if not a cure to a problem, as he was advised to consult Billy on one occasion, with positive results.]

Billy was something of a recluse in his later years but his friends knew that his one wish was to take some cider to his grave with him, to see him through the next stage of existence. When the time came, Billy's friends convinced the funeral director, who knew Billy well enough himself, that they should respect Billy's lifelong avowed intention. With due reverence and solemnity, Billy was carried to his grave by his friends but few knew that the coffin contained a cask of cider to satisfy the needs of the departed countryman. One thing is quite certain: Billy's request was not an isolated one. The old customs do still survive.

[As a grisly footnote, it is said that if one buys items once belonging to a recently deceased person, those items could be expected to mildew; the posessions of the dead always turning mouldy, as does a grave.]

In all areas of the West Country, ghosts, spirits and spectres can be encountered. There are numerous stories; some drive in coaches from place to place, pursuing an eternal quest, some tackle never-ending tasks, some perpetually patrol premises or places associated with their worldly existence, while others appear to be earth-bound by - sometimes horrific - events of ages long gone.

To come across a 'ghost' in a supposedly haunted castle is one thing, but to find an un-dead spirit in its own coffin is, surely, another matter altogether.

The Rev Baring Gould wrote in his *Book of Folk-lore* of the circumstances in which his grandfather encountered his own deceased relative, a lady who was not so much 'haunting' anywhere, but was more simply found to be 'in residence' in her own coffin. He wrote:

> *In 1832 my grandfather renovated Lew Trenchard Church. He swept away the rood-screen and the carved oak benches and repewed the church. The carpenter employed opened the vault of old Madame Gould, the grandmother of my grandfather.*
>
> *She had been a notable woman, and he thought he would like to see her. It was night, and he had his lantern. I tell the tale as he told it me. When he opened her coffin she sat up, and a light streamed from her above that of his lantern. He was so panic-stricken that he fled the church, and ran home a distance of a quarter of a mile. And as he told me, she followed him, and he knew that, because her shadow went before him the whole way. Arrived at his home, he dashed in and jumped into the bed beside his wife, who was ill, and both saw Madame standing before them, with a light shining about her, which gradually faded.*
>
> *He told me this story himself, with all the sincerity of a man who is speaking the truth. The next day he found his extinguished lantern where he had left it.*

The interest that Baring-Gould had in what might be called nowadays, the paranormal, is well established, and his work is generally a reliable record of events, customs or traditions. The man who, while at Horbury, wrote 'Now the Day is Over', 'Onward, Christian Soldiers', and other now well loved hymns, was not a man to confuse fact with fantasy, even when re-telling a tale told to him by his grandfather.

Clearly, the lady had long been deceased, but when that gentleman opened her coffin she was 'alive' in some mysterious manner; or at least, she was not dead.

MUSEUM OF WITCHCRAFT

The museum in Boscastle, in north-east Cornwall, is, as far as we are aware, the only museum in the UK solely devoted to exhibiting items related to witchcraft and to encouraging a further and wider understanding of the entire subject. Museum owners Roger King and his partner Liz Crow both profess to be working on the periphery of the present day Craft and state that their objective is to provide accurate, reliable and interesting information rather than to present commercialised misrepresentation and titillation.

When the priests of old grafted their new-found beliefs on to ancient understanding and clothed the Gods of Nature with a new religion, they laid the foundations for the holocaust that took the lives of thousands of men and women who were condemned to death as witches and provided a continuing way in which the few can influence the majority.

Never, at any time in the history of humankind, more than at the present, has there been such a desire to understand the past. For those who want to cultivate the fear of 'witchcraft', the museum will be a whipping post.

For those who wish to learn of the past, the museum is a repository of fact. For those who want to understand the wisdom of our ancestors, the museum may indicate the way.

AN EPITAPH FOR ALL WITCHES

In Exeter, during the penultimate decade of the seventeenth century, the last sentences of death were passed upon English witches. People were tried elsewhere for crimes associated with witchcraft, Northampton in 1705 and again eleven years later, in Huntingdon in 1716, but there is no reliable evidence to show that execution was the penalty for any who stood before the court at those times. Margaret Young was tried for witchcraft in the west of England in 1689 and found guilty. She was sentenced to death by Sir Robert Atkynsn but was later reprieved.

Among the last witches to be executed were the three women from Bideford, Susanna Edwards, Temperance Lloyd and Mary Trembles who, on 25 August 1682, were taken through the streets of Exeter to Heavitree, the place of execution, and there they were hanged.

Less than two years later the execution of such unfortunate victims of society, male or female, ended when Alice Molland became the last woman condemned to death in England for practising witchcraft. At her trial in Exeter she was found guilty of being a witch, and sentenced to death on 20 March 1684. Alice, like so many before her, hanged at Heavitree.

To the memory of these four women a plaque has been placed on the ruined wall of Rougemont Castle, close by the court in which they received their sentences.

A fitting epitaph for them, and all witches, had been written almost a quarter of a century earlier by playwrights Rowley, Dekker and Ford, words that were spoken as a soliloquy in a play by a character who was considered to be a witch:

Why should the envious world
Throw all their scandalous malice upon me,
'Cause I am poor, deformed, and ignorant,
And like a bow buckled and bent together,
By some more strong in mischiefs than myself?
Must I for that be made a common sink
For all the filth and rubbish of men's tongues
To fall and run into? Some call me witch;
And, being ignorant of myself, they go
About to teach me how to be one.
This they enforce upon me. . . .

Further Reading

Baring-Gould, Rev S *The Book of Vampires* (Smith, Elder & Co 1865)
- *Curgenven* (1893)
Crossing, W *Western Antiquary* (1884 ed)
Davies, R Trevor *Four Centuries of Witch Beliefs* (1947)
Farquharson-Coe, A *Hants & Dorset Witchcraft* (H E Warne 1975)
Freeman, A E *English Towns & Districts* (1879-1887)
Fuller, Dr Thomas *The Church History of Britain*
Gent, Frank *The Trial of the Bideford Witches* (published by the author
  1983. New edition to be issued. Contact Rougemont Museum, Exeter)
Hardy, Thomas *The Return of the Native* (1878)
Hole, Christina *Witchcraft in England* (B T Batsford 1977)
Hone, William *The Table Book* (Thomas Tegg 1827)
- *The Everyday Book* (Thomas Tegg 1841)
- *The Year Book* (Thomas Tegg 1845)
Kendrick, T D *The Druids* (Methuen & Co 1927)
Kitteridge, G L *Witchcraft in Old & New England* (New York 1929)
Martin, B.W. *The Dictionary of the Occult* (Rider & Co 1979)
Radford, E & M A *Who Killed Dick Whittington?* (Andrew Melrose Ltd)
Radford, K *Fire Burn* (Michael O'Mara Books Ltd 1989)
Robbins, R H *The Encyclopaedia of Witchcraft & Demonology* (Hamlyn,
  1979)
Rutherford, Ward *Celtic Lore* (The Aquarian Press 1993)
Scot, Reginald *Discoverie of Witchcraft* (1584, reprinted 1964)
Sprenger, J & Kramer, H *Malleus Maleficarum* (1486, Folio Society ed
  1968)
St Leger-Gordon, Ruth E *The Witchcraft and Folklore of Dartmoor*
  (1965, reprinted Peninsula Press 1994)
Summers, M *The History of Witchcraft and Demonology* (1926, Senate-
  Studio editions 1994)
Thompson, Janet A *Wives, Widows, Witches and Bitches: Women in 17th
  Century Devon* (Peter Lang Publishing 1993)
Valiente, Doreen *An ABC of Witchcraft Past & Present* (Robert Hale
  1973)